Receivership Manual

Third Edition

Martin Iredale FCA
Christopher Hughes FCA

Tolley Publishing Company Limited

A BENN GROUP PUBLICATION

First published 1978
Second edition 1983
Third edition 1987

Published by
Tolley Publishing Company Limited
Tolley House, 17 Scarbrook Road
Croydon Surrey CR0 1SQ England
01-686 9141

Typeset by C Leggett & Son, Mitcham, Surrey

Printed in the United Kingdom
by the Whitefriars Press Limited
Tonbridge, Kent

Preface

This third edition of the manual has been brought about by the Insolvency Act 1986, the Company Directors Disqualification Act 1986 and the raft of supporting legislation contained in numerous statutory instruments.

It is as well for insolvency practitioners, as they are now known, to be familiar with all the changes brought about and the new burdens placed on them regarding the bonding procedures and the manner in which insolvency proceedings are now to be conducted.

All these matters, insofar as they impact on the administrative receiver, are discussed in detail. Directors too must be aware of their responsibilities and we have devoted a section of this manual to the obligation of administrative receivers to consider and, if necessary, report on the conduct of directors. We have also discussed the role of the administrator and the effect of a petition for the making of an administration order on secured and unsecured creditors and the administrative receiver himself.

We must acknowledge with thanks the considerable work carried out by Michael Denison from the Cork Gully technical department and the assistance given by Pamela Moore without whose dexterity on her word processor the publication of this manual would have been put back many weeks. Finally, we are grateful to the Department of Employment, The Solicitors' Law Stationery Society plc and Fourmat Publishing for permission to reproduce various published forms.

Cork Gully
London EC2
July 1987

Martin Iredale
Christopher Hughes

Contents

Contents

Contents

RECEIVERSHIP INSTRUCTIONS AND MEMORANDA

Abbreviations

Statutes

Companies Act 1985 (C.6)	CA
Company Directors Disqualification Act 1986 (C.26)	CDDA
Employment Protection Act 1975 (C.71)	EPA
Employment Protection (Consolidation) Act 1978 (C.44)	EP(C)A
Income and Corporation Taxes Act 1970 (C.10)	ICTA
Insolvency Act 1986 (C.45)	IA
Insolvency Practitioners Regulations 1986 [S.I. 1986 No. 1995]	IPR
Insolvency Practitioners (Amendment) Regulations 1986 [S.I. 1986 No. 2247]	IP(A)R
Insolvency Rules 1986 [S.I. 1986 No. 1925]	IR
Law of Property Act 1925 (C.20)	LPA
Social Security Pensions Act 1975 (C.60)	SSPA
The Transfer of Undertakings (Protection of Employment) Regulations 1981 [S.I. 1981 No. 1794]	TU(PE)R

Cases

AC	Appeal Cases (3rd series)
Ad & El	Adolphus & Ellis
All ER	All England Law Reports
App. Cas	Appeal Cases (2nd series)
B & Ald	Barnewall & Alderson
BCLC	Butterworth's Company Law Cases
CB (NS)	Common Bench, New Series
Ch	Chancery Division (3rd series)
Ch.D	Chancery Division (2nd series)
CLR	Commonwealth Law Reports
Cowp	Cowper
Cox CC	Cox's Criminal Cases
E & B	Ellis & Blackburn
E & E	Ellis & Ellis
KB	King's Bench
LJQB	Law Journal Queen's Bench
Lloyds Rep	Lloyds List Law Reports
Mer	Merivale
Mod. Rep	Modern Reports
QB	Queen's Bench
SJ	Solicitors' Journal
SLT	Scots Law Times
TLR	Times Law Reports
Willes	Willes (ed. Durnford)
WLR	Weekly Law Reports

Table of Statutes

Table of Cases

Chapter 1

Preliminary Considerations

1.1   The objective of this manual is to give practical advice in solving the principal problems which are likely to face a person who has been appointed administrative receiver of a company under a debenture with power to manage a company's business. This first chapter comments on directors' responsibilities and the options open to them when it appears to them that the company is insolvent. It also considers briefly the difficulties that the directors are likely to face if they do not take appropriate action. Chapter 2 is concerned with insolvency practitioners and the statutory obligations imposed on them in order that they can accept appointments. It also covers various types of receiverships other than administrative receiverships. The remaining chapters and appendices cover in detail the practical and statutory matters with which the administrative receiver is likely to be concerned.

Directors' Responsibilities

1.2   It is important to consider at an early stage the position of directors and the burdens placed on them by the Companies Act 1985, the Insolvency Act 1986 and the Company Directors Disqualification Act 1986. If the directors conclude (or should be aware) that the company is insolvent they must take 'every step with a view to minimising the potential loss to the company's creditors . . . that they ought to take'. (IA s 214(3)).

If they do not do so and the company ultimately goes into insolvent liquidation then it is possible for the liquidator to apply to the court under the 'wrongful trading' provisions for an order that the directors make such contribution to the company's assets as the court thinks proper (IA s 214(1)). The term 'directors' is also deemed to include shadow directors whose role is defined in the Act as 'a person in accordance with whose directions or instructions the directors of the company are accustomed to act' (IA s 251).

The Alternatives

1.3   It is not the intention to go into detail as to the various options available but an insolvency practitioner consulted by the directors will probably consider the benefits or otherwise of the following:

(a)   a voluntary arrangement
(b)   an administration order
(c)   administrative receivership, and
(d)   liquidation

Obviously, the particular circumstance in which the company finds itself is likely to determine the route down which the insolvency practitioner will proceed. In the first instance it is important for the practitioner not to prejudge a situation but to keep an open mind as to which procedure to recommend. This manual concentrates on the appointment of an administrative receiver and gives details in later chapters as to when and how such an appointment can be made. The other available procedures are considered in detail in companion volumes to this manual.

The Broad View of an Administrative Receiver's Function

1.4   Administrative receivership demands that a swift and searching appraisal of the financial position and future prospects of a company be made. The administrative receiver will be in sole command. His problems may be acute and the pressures upon him intense during the first few weeks. It is essential, however, that the day-to-day problems should not be allowed to impede the progress of the examination of the overall position and so delay the conclusions of that examination. The administrative receiver is an investigating accountant with power to implement his recommendations forthwith and the sole chief executive.

1.5   The appointment of an administrative receiver to a company does not necessarily mean that the company's activities will come to an end. As soon as possible after his appointment, the administrative receiver should consider whether there is any alternative to ceasing to trade and realising the assets at break-up values. He should ask himself the following questions:

(a)   Can the company, with the administrative receiver in control, trade through its present crisis without prejudice to the position of the debenture holder and creditors?

(b)   Is it possible to dispose of non-essential assets to raise funds for repayment of the debenture?

(c)   Is it possible to close down unprofitable activities quickly, so as to salvage the rest of the business?

(d)   Can any section of the company be sold to raise funds whilst the remainder of the business is left intact?

(e)   Can any financial reorganisation or reconstruction be put into place to enable a repayment of the debenture, or provide adequate security to the debenture holder?

(f)   Should the business continue trading for a limited time so as to enable the administrative receiver to attempt to sell the assets at going-concern valuations?

(g)   Should the business, goodwill and assets be passed down to a newly formed wholly-owned subsidiary, so as to facilitate the subsequent sale of the business as a going concern?

1.6   As in all business enterprises, it is important that the administrative receiver, once he has decided on his strategy, should not be deflected from his main purpose, e.g. by pressure from interested parties. His powers are considerable and he should use them.

Chapter 2

The Administrative Receiver and Other Receivership Appointments

2.1   An important feature of the Insolvency Act 1986 is that appointments as administrative receiver can only be taken by individuals who hold an appropriate licence from either the professional body of which they are a member or directly from the Department of Trade and Industry (IA s 390(2)). It is a criminal offence for anyone to act as administrative receiver unless he is qualified to act as an insolvency practitioner in relation to the company (IA s 389(1)).

Bonding Requirements – General Penalty

2.2   The insolvency practitioner, before taking any appointment, must be able to demonstrate that he has a bond with a 'general penalty sum' of £250,000 (IPR 10(1)(a)). The bond itself will be held by whichever relevant body has licensed the insolvency practitioner. It is also a requirement of the Insolvency Rules 12.8(1) that the appointor satisfies himself that his appointee has such security for the proper performance of his functions.

Bonding Requirements – Specific Penalty

2.3   In addition to the general penalty bond of £250,000, the insolvency practitioner who accepts an appointment as administrative receiver must obtain for each appointment a 'certificate of specific penalty' under his bond as soon as reasonably possible (IPR 10(1)(b)). The bond must be up to a value 'equivalent to that part of the assets . . . which would appear to be available for the unsecured creditors of the company whether in respect of the preferential debts of the company or otherwise'. There is a minimum of £5,000, and a maximum of £5,000,000 (IPR Sch 2 and IP(A)R 2). 'Unsecured creditors' are defined in such a way as to include preferential creditors.

The valuation is made at the date of the appointment so that the costs of the administrative receivership should be ignored. If at any time after the issue of the certificate it appears that the penalty sum of the bond is inadequate then a further certificate of specific penalty must be obtained. (IPR 10(1)(c)). In every case a copy of the certificate of penalty (or any further certificate where additional cover is found necessary) must be delivered to the Registrar of Companies within 14 days of receipt of the certificate(s). (IPR 12(1)).

The Statutory Record – Maintenance

2.4   Administrative receivers are required to maintain a record in respect of each of their appointments (IPR 15). Where two or more practitioners are appointed jointly, each must maintain a separate record. The record must be kept in the form as set out in Appendix H.1.

The Statutory Record – Inspection

2.5   The practitioner must notify the body from whom he obtained his licence of the place where his records are kept (IPR 17). They can then be inspected, on the giving of reasonable notice, by:

(a)   any duly authorised representative of the licensing body, or
(b)   the Secretary of State for Trade and Industry. (IPR 16).

2.6   The record relating to any particular appointment must be kept for a minimum of ten years from:

(a)   the date of the practitioner's release or discharge as office holder, or
(b)   the date on which the certificate of specific penalty expired or otherwise ceased to have effect,
whichever is the later (IPR 18).

Appointments under Fixed and Floating Charges

2.7   The 'administrative receiver' is defined as 'a receiver or manager of the whole (or substantially the whole) of a company's property appointed by or on behalf of the holders of any debentures of the company secured by a charge which, as created, was a floating charge or by such a charge and one or more other securities (IA s 29(2)(a) and (b)); or a person who would be such a receiver or manager but for the appointment of some other person as the receiver of part of the company's property'.

The appointment, except on the rare occasions when it takes place under a Court order (see paragraphs 2.10 – 2.17 below), is made under an instrument of appointment executed by the debenture holder. This is the administrative receiver's authority to act and can be produced when required, together with the debenture, as evidence of his capacity. The object of an administrative receivership is to obtain repayment for the debenture holder as quickly as possible within the overall context of the administrative receiver's powers and authority and with due regard to the rights of other creditors and the shareholders.

2.8   An administrative receiver will generally be appointed in one or more of the following circumstances:

(a)   The borrower fails to comply with the terms of the debenture concerning repayment of principal and interest.
(b)   Part or all of the principal is properly recalled by the debenture holder and the borrower fails to comply.
(c)   The limit of a secured banking advance or other borrowing limit is exceeded and the borrowing is not reduced within a stipulated period.
(d)   The provisions of the debenture or trust deed are in some other way breached by the borrower. (A technical breach can normally be rectified by agreement).

2.9   The debenture holder's security is usually in the form of fixed and floating charges on the assets of the company. It is, however, possible for the security to be simply a fixed charge or a floating charge. The following matters are, therefore, of the utmost importance and must be considered at the commencement of any company receivership:

(a)   Under a fixed charge a receiver will normally have no power to manage the business.
(b)   Under a floating charge the appointment may be made as 'receiver' or 'administrative receiver'. A receiver cannot be appointed with the powers of an administrative receiver unless the debenture deed contains a provision giving the necessary powers to the debenture holder to make such an appointment.
(c)   A receiver appointed solely as 'receiver' has, however, power to manage if such right is given to him by the debenture deed and the deed contains a charge on the goodwill or business of the company.

Other Receivership Appointments

Court-Appointed Receivers

2.10 The Courts can appoint receivers in a variety of circumstances, as certain industrial disputes in the early nineteen-eighties made clear. Most commonly, perhaps, they appoint receivers:

(a) to enforce charges in favour of mortgagees or other secured creditors; or
(b) to control assets pending the outcome of litigation.

2.11 The prospective receiver will normally be approached by the solicitors acting for the mortgagees (or one of the parties to the litigation) before an application is made to the court for an order of appointment. The terms of the order the court is to be asked to make must be considered very carefully, as *the receiver will be able to do only those things he is authorised to do by the order and no more*. The order will not necessarily give the receiver power to sell the property, even if he is appointed to protect the interests of a mortgagee.

2.12 A receiver may be appointed over partnership assets pending resolution of a dispute among the partners themselves. He should consider, together with the solicitors to the parties, the extent to which the partnership can continue trading. Does the order allow the receiver or the partners themselves to operate bank accounts for this purpose? Particular care must be taken with trades and professions which can only be conducted by those having particular licences or professional qualifications.

2.13 Where a receiver is appointed pending the outcome of litigation, he is appointed to protect the interests of all parties even though he may have been appointed at the instigation of one only. He must comply strictly with the terms of the order of appointment and not favour one party over another.

2.14 A receiver appointed by the court is not himself a party to the action and therefore has no *locus standi* to apply for any supplementary orders that may be required, unless such power is given to him in the order of appointment or subsequently. A person invited to act as receiver under a court appointment should try to ensure that the order does give him power to apply to the court where necessary.

2.15 Unless such power has been given, any application to the court must be made by the solicitors acting for one or more of the parties. This does not apply, however, to any order sought by the receiver himself to enable him to enforce the powers granted to him by the appointment (e.g. to require debts to be paid to him). The receiver is an officer of the court and any attempted interference with him in the conduct of his duties constitutes contempt of court.

2.16 The court must fix the receiver's remuneration and discharge the appointment. The basis of remuneration and circumstances of discharge should normally be agreed with the secured creditor, or the parties to the action, beforehand.

2.17 A receiver appointed by the court does not have any right of indemnity against the parties themselves. (*Evans v Clayhope Properties Ltd*, The Times 10 November 1986, and [1987] 1 WLR 225).

If, therefore, the assets over which the receiver is to be appointed are considered insufficient to indemnify him against any liabilities he might incur, he should seek an indemnity from one or more of the parties before agreeing to nomination.

Receiver Appointed by Mortgagee (LPA Receiver)

2.18 A receiver may be appointed by a mortgagee of property if the power is included in the terms of the mortgage deed. However, Section 109(1) of the Law of

Property Act 1925 ('LPA') stops a mortgagee appointing a receiver until the mortgagee's power of sale has become operative. The power of sale will arise:

(a)   in accordance with any specific provisions in the mortgage itself; or
(b)   under Section 103 of the LPA, if:
  (i)   a demand for a payment due under the mortgage has been served on the mortgagor and three months or more have elapsed without payment having been made,
  (ii)   interest remains unpaid for two months or more after it fell due, or
  (iii)   there has been a breach of any provision contained either in the mortgage or the LPA.

2.19   The receiver must be appointed by a written instrument, which may be either signed or sealed. The receiver's appointment takes effect when he receives and accepts the instrument of appointment even if it was signed or executed earlier (*Cripps (Pharmaceuticals) Ltd v Wickenden* [1973] 1 WLR 944). (LPA s 109(1)). The receiver is deemed to be agent for the mortgagor (i.e. the debtor), who is solely responsible for the receiver's acts and defaults unless the mortgage itself provides otherwise (LPA s 109(2)).

2.20   The receiver does not necessarily take physical possession of the property over which he has been appointed, but he is entitled to all income, rent and other benefits flowing from the property and shall instruct all tenants to pay their rent (including any arrears) to him. He may enforce his right to receive the income by taking legal action or levying distress in the name of the mortgagor or mortgagee, should it be necessary.

2.21   The LPA confers no management powers on the receiver. The mortgagee may delegate to the receiver in writing the powers to grant leases or accept surrenders of leases.

2.22   The receiver must:

(a)   insure the property, if directed by the mortgagee to do so;
(b)   execute necessary or proper repairs, if directed by the mortgagee to do so; and
(c)   apply money received in accordance with section 109(8) of the LPA i.e.:

  (i)   in discharge of all rent, rates, taxes and outgoings affecting the mortgaged property,
  (ii)   in keeping down all annual sums and other payments of interest on a principal sum having priority to the mortgage in respect of which he is receiver,
  (iii)   in payment of his commission and of the premiums of fire, life or other insurance, if any, properly payable under the mortgage deed or under the Act and the cost of executing necessary or proper repairs directed in writing by the mortgagee,
  (iv)   in payment of interest accruing due in respect of any principal money due under the mortgage,
  (v)   in or towards the discharge of principal monies if so directed in writing by the mortgagee,
  (vi)   in paying the residue to the person who, but for the receiver's possession, would have been entitled to receive the income or is otherwise entitled to the mortgaged property.

2.23   The receiver's remuneration is fixed by agreement with the mortgagee as specified in the appointment *but*, except with the leave of the court, is not to exceed 5% of sums received. This 5% maximum is intended to include all costs, charges and expenses. In *Marshall v Cottingham* [1981] 3 WLR 235 it was decided that agents' fees and expenses, conveyancing costs and caretaking costs prior to sale were *not* part of the costs, charges and expenses to be included in the 5%. As remuneration is to be retained by the receiver out of monies coming into his hands in effect the cost is borne by the mortgagor if there is a surplus after meeting all claims by the mortgagee.

2.24 It is not necessary for a receiver (who is not an administrative receiver) to be qualified to act as an insolvency practitioner nor does such a receiver have the power to require public utilities to continue supplies notwithstanding the non-payment of arrears.

Chapter 3

The Legal Aspects of the Appointment of an Administrative Receiver

3.1   The effectiveness of the receiver will depend to a very large extent on a knowledge of the law which defines his powers and responsibilities under different types of charge. An attempt is therefore made in this chapter to group together the main legal aspects of the appointment of a receiver.

Types of Charge

3.2   A fixed charge is a direct charge on specific assets detailed in the debenture and is therefore in the nature of a mortgage. A floating charge, however, can be regarded as a charge coupled with permission to the company to continue to deal with its assets until the charge crystallises, for example upon the appointment of an administrative receiver, or by the company ceasing to carry on business.

3.3   A fixed charge on any assets prevents the company from dealing with such assets by way of sale or mortgage, without the consent of the debenture holder. With a floating charge, no such consent is required, although there is usually a clause in the debenture prohibiting the creation of prior charges. Another important point to remember is that preferential creditors have priority over the debenture holders with regard to assets covered by a floating charge. Many modern debenture stock trust deeds contain provisions restricting the powers of the company to dispose of its assets. If the company has transferred assets in breach of such a clause, and the transferee knew the transfer was in breach, it is possible (though it has never been decided) that the receiver would have rights against the transferee.

3.4   Fixed charges are normally taken over 'immovable' assets, such as land and buildings and plant and machinery. In recent years, however, there has been a growing tendency for banks and others to take fixed charges over 'present and future book debts'. The creation of a fixed charge on what might be considered to be a 'floating' asset has been for many years a controversial issue. This issue was considered in the case of *Siebe Gorman & Co Ltd v Barclays Bank Ltd* [1979] 2 Lloyd's Rep 142 where Mr Justice Slade concluded 'that the debenture on its true construction conferred on the bank a specific charge on all future book debts and that the rights of the bank as a specific chargee attached in equity to their proceeds as soon as they were paid'. In that case the proceeds of the debts were paid into an account with the bank, so that the bank could control any dealings with cash proceeds. The question of whether a charge is fixed or floating will usually depend on the extent to which the chargee permits the company to deal without specific control. The proceeds of sales made by a company after the appointment of a receiver cannot be deemed to be covered by such a charge.

3.5   The receiver is not required to keep separate accounts or to maintain separate funds if there are both fixed and floating charges in favour of the same person. However, he should see that an accurate division is made between the assets realised under the fixed charge and the floating charge in the receipts and payments accounts issued to the Registrar of Companies, to the debenture holders, and to the company since only amounts realised under a floating charge will be available for preferential creditors (see paragraph 8.20 below). Great care is necessary in these circumstances in dealing with those items e.g. fixtures and movable plant and machinery, where there may be doubt as to whether they are covered by the fixed charge or not.

Validity of Charge

3.6   All floating charges created by a company and many other types of charge created by a company (including charges on land) are void against the liquidator and any creditor of the company unless they are registered, with the Registrar of Companies, within twenty-one days of their creation (CA s 395(1)).

3.7   Charges can also be invalid against the liquidator or administrator in the following circumstances:

(a)   A fixed charge is invalid if it is created at a time in the period of six months, or in the case of a connected person two years, ending with the onset of insolvency and also that it was created either when the company could not pay its debts or as a result of creating the charge, became unable to pay its debts (IA s 240(1) and (2)). It must be noted that in the case of a charge being created in favour of a connected person then the company will be deemed to be unable to pay its debts unless the contrary is shown (IA s 240(2)).

(b)   A floating charge is invalid if it is created at a time in the period of twelve months, or in the case of a connected person two years, ending with the onset of insolvency and, where the chargee was not a connected person, the company was unable to pay its debts or became unable as a result of creating the charge (IA s 245(3) and (4)).

(c)   Both fixed and floating charges are invalid if created between the presentation of a petition for an administration order and the making of such an order (IA s 240(1) and 245(3)(c)).

For the purposes of (a) and (b) above 'onset of insolvency' means either the date of the presentation of the petition on which an administration order was made or in the case of a company going into liquidation at any other time, the date of the commencement of the winding up (IA s 240(3)(a) and (b)).

Floating charges subject to avoidance under paragraph 3.7(b) above will only be valid to the extent of the aggregate of money paid or goods or services supplied to the company at the time of or after creation of the charge, payments made by the chargeholder in reduction of debts due by the company and any interest arising on the above amounts (IA s 245(2)).

3.8   It should be noted that payments made by a bank to a third party, in respect of cheques drawn by the company, may constitute cash paid to the company within the meaning of IA s 245. A floating charge in favour of a bank may, therefore, be valid even though it was created within twelve months of a liquidation and although prima facie no new cash had been advanced to the company (*Re Yeovil Glove Company Ltd* [1965] Ch 148).

3.9   Even if a charge may become invalid if the company goes into liquidation or becomes subject to an administration order within twelve months of its creation, it will remain valid unless and until the liquidator or administrator applies successfully for the charge to be declared by the courts to be invalid. Until such an event occurs, any administrative receiver appointed will be entitled to act and to pay to the charge holder any sums becoming available under the charge (*Mace Builders (Glasgow) v Lunn* [1985] 3 WLR 465).

Mode of Appointment

3.10 The method by which the administrative receiver is to be appointed will normally be specified in the charge document. Most standard bank debentures state that an administrative receiver may be appointed by a written instrument signed by a duly authorised bank official. If two or more people are to be appointed to act as joint administrative receivers in relation to a company, the instrument of appointment must state whether acts are to be done by one or more or all of them (IA s 231).

Acceptance of Appointment

3.11 The appointment must be accepted no later than the end of the business day following the day on which the instrument of appointment was received by or on behalf of the appointee but, subject to such acceptance, takes effect from the time it was received (IA s 33(1)). An appointment can be accepted simply by giving the appointor oral intimation of the acceptance, but the time that such intimation is given must be noted. In the case of a joint appointment, each appointee must accept although the same person may be authorised to receive and accept the appointment on behalf of both or all the appointees.

3.12 Written confirmation of the acceptance of the appointment must be given to the appointor within seven days of receipt of the instrument of appointment (IR 3.1(1)). The written confirmation must:

(a)   be given by the appointee or someone duly authorised by him (IR 3.1(3)); and
(b)   state the time and date the appointment was received and the time and date it was accepted (IR 3.1(4)).

A specimen confirmation of appointment is shown in appendix I.1.

In the case of a joint appointment, each appointee must confirm acceptance of appointment and the appointment is not effective until both or all appointees have done so (IR 3.1(2)).

3.13 The chargeholder must give the Registrar notice of the appointment within seven days (see appendix H.13); the chargeholder should *always* be asked to confirm that he has done this (CA s 405(1)).

Validity of Appointment

3.14 In all cases it is desirable for the administrative receiver to seek the advice immediately of a firm of solicitors who act neither for the chargeholder nor the company as to the validity of the appointment (see appendix J.4). If for some reason the appointment is found to be invalid then the court may order that the putative appointee be indemnified by the purported appointor against any liability arising out of the invalidity of the appointment (IA s 34).

Effect of Petition for Administration Order

3.15 If a petition for an administration order is presented to the court, notice must be given to any person entitled to appoint an administrative receiver (IA s 9(2)). That chargeholder can then effectively veto the appointment of the administrator by appointing his own administrative receiver before the court hearing. The court will then dismiss the petition unless either the chargeholder consented to the making of the order or the court was satisfied that the charge itself was liable to be upset for some reason.

Similarly, if an administrative receiver has already been appointed when a petition is presented to the court, the petition will be dismissed unless the appointor has consented to the making of the order (IA s 9(3)(a)).

3.16 If the administration order is made, any administrative receiver must vacate office (IA s 11(1)(b)). Thereafter while the order remains in force an administrative receiver cannot be appointed (IA s 11(3)(b)).

3.17 When a receiver vacates office under paragraph 3.16 above he is entitled to his remuneration and expenses and costs properly incurred from the proceeds of sale of any property in his custody or control in priority to his appointee (IA s 11(4)(a) and (b)). The receiver, where leaving office under paragraph 3.16, has no duty to pay the preferential creditors (IA s 11(5)).

Powers, Status, and Responsibility of the Receiver

3.18 Modern floating charges usually confer extensive powers on a receiver and they are deemed to include all powers specified in Schedule 1 to the Act (see appendix C) except where these are inconsistent with any of the provisions in the charge documents. If he is in any doubt, the receiver should take legal advice on the extent of his powers. The receiver should also consider taking advantage of the provisions of IA s 35, under which a receiver appointed out of court can apply to the court for directions. A receiver can resort to this machinery at any time if he is faced with a problem that appears to him, after taking legal advice, to have no unequivocal solution. In such cases, a summons is issued by the receiver, supported by affidavit as to the facts and seeking the court's approval of a particular course of action. The court will give direction if it requires further evidence in order to consider the problem.

3.19 The receiver is deemed to have the power to carry on the business and he may do so without being specifically appointed manager provided the deed contains a charge on the goodwill or business of the company. The powers of the receiver supersede those of the directors so far as the management of the business is concerned. The assets do not vest in the receiver but he takes possession of those assets covered by the charge and deals with them according to his powers and responsibilities.

3.20 The receiver is deemed to be the company's agent unless and until the company goes into liquidation (IA s 44(1)(a)). However, he is personally liable on any contract entered into by him in the performance of his function except where the contract otherwise provides. He is also liable on any contract of employment adopted by him although he is not to be taken as having adopted a contract of employment by reason of anything done or omitted to be done within fourteen days after his appointment (IA s 44(1)(b) and 44(2)). He should therefore send a letter to all employees as soon as possible, but in any event less than fourteen days after his appointment, advising them that he is *not* adopting their contracts but will make funds available to the company to continue paying their wages (see appendix J.15). He is entitled to an indemnity from the assets of the company provided the contract is not entered into without authority (IA s 44(1)(c)).

3.21 In some circumstances it may be preferable for the mortgagee to sell important assets such as the undertaking of the company, or the immovable property of the company under the mortgagee's power of sale, rather than for the receiver to sell these assets. The advantages of the mortgagee selling are as follows:

(a)   A sale by a mortgagee under the statutory power of sale overrides any second or subsequent charges or encumbrances on the property. A sale by a receiver does not necessarily have this effect.

(b)   The potential liability on any covenants or warranties that the receiver gives on selling the assets may delay his handing over to a mortgagee the proceeds of the receivership. Where the mortgagee sells, any such liability will attach to the mortgagee and will not therefore prevent the receiver accounting to him.

(c)   The statutory right of a mortgagee to sell is a well-established legal right. The power of a receiver to sell, even after liquidation and thus the cessation of his agency, has been clarified (*Barrows v Chief Land Registrar*, The Times 20 October 1977). It was held that the winding-up order terminated his agency but did not terminate his power to execute or sign documents as receiver in the name of the company. Any doubt however has been removed by the Insolvency Act 1986 as the powers conferred on him are set out in Schedule 1 to the Act (see appendix C).

The Liquidator's Rights to Challenge the Receiver's Actions

3.22 The receiver is accountable to the company in the person of its directors or liquidator for any balance in his hands after repayment of amounts due under the debenture. In the event of a liquidator being appointed, it is usual for him to examine the validity of the receiver's dealings to satisfy himself that no improper transactions have been entered into by the receiver which may be detrimental to the general body of creditors. However, if the receiver has acted in good faith, prudently, and within the scope of his authority, he cannot be successfully challenged by a liquidator. Examples of this are:

(a) A receiver may pay an unsecured creditor where non-payment would place the assets of the company in serious jeopardy, e.g. where a supplier of an essential component refuses to deliver to the receiver unless his outstanding account is paid and non-delivery of the component would certainly cause greater loss than the amount of the payment, assuming that the goods cannot be obtained elsewhere. (It should be remembered that it is often possible to persuade a supplier to continue deliveries on the understanding that he will be paid for his supplies to the receiver. Payment of one unsecured creditor is likely to lead to demands and threats of non-supply from others who want to be treated similarly, and these may cause great difficulties for the receiver. A receiver should therefore make every endeavour to avoid paying unsecured creditors, and should only do so where assets overall would undoubtedly show a net gain, and there is no practical alternative.)

(b) A sale of a particular asset at a price below the best offer for that asset is justified if such a sale forms part of a larger deal more advantageous to the debenture holder.

(c) Contracts made by the company prior to the appointment of a receiver need not be performed by the receiver, although this may give rise to large unsecured claims against the company. If losses are being made on such contracts by the company to the detriment of the debenture holder, the receiver's action in not performing the contract cannot be effectively challenged.

3.23 Preferential creditors rank in priority to the debenture holder against those assets covered by a floating charge and in extreme cases the receiver may have to ask the debenture holder for an indemnity with regard to the preferential creditors before he continues to trade. If a receiver decides to carry on the business and ultimately does so at a loss, then he may well be personally liable to the extent to which he uses stock and other assets under the floating charge which would otherwise have been available for the preferential creditors (*Westminster City Council v Haste* [1950] Ch 442).

Recapitulation of the Receiver's Principal Duties

3.24 In summary, the receiver's prime duty is that of repaying the debenture holder and, in priority over a floating charge, the preferential creditors. He must not make unnecessary losses and so reduce the assets available for preferential creditors. In his actions, he should show the degree of care expected of a prudent businessman. For example, in selling assets, he should take the same care such a businessman would take to attract prospective buyers and obtain the best price for the assets. The receiver should constantly consider whether his actions are likely to be regarded as unnecessarily detrimental to the unsecured creditors and shareholders, but he must at all times act as his prime duty requires.

Chapter 4

Immediate Steps to be Taken Following Appointment

4.1   A receiver may well have investigated the affairs of the company prior to his appointment. If he is appointed under a debenture where he has no knowledge of the affairs of the business he will often be suddenly confronted with operational and administrative problems which are entirely strange to him. In these circumstances, having ensured that his appointment is valid and having ascertained the exact powers conferred upon him by the debenture, he should prepare a schedule of matters which require immediate attention and a programme for his further course of action (see appendices A and B).

4.2   In an earlier passage (see paragraph 1.5 above) it was emphasised that the key decision, after appointment, is whether to keep the business going so as to sell it. The considerations behind this decision are spelt out in chapter 6, together with advice on how best to attempt to preserve the benefit of past tax losses for the potential purchaser of the business.

Meetings with Directors and Senior Management

4.3   Almost invariably, the receiver's first step will be to meet the directors and senior management, in order to advise them of his appointment and of the legal and practical consequences. He will require their assistance in obtaining information about the company, and in the implementation of controls and the general administration of the business in the event that trading is continued.

4.4   The position of the directors of a company where a receiver has been appointed is as follows:

(a)   Their powers in relation to the management of the company are suspended although their statutory obligations continue (see paragraph 3.19 above). The directors should be advised of their obligations in this respect (see appendix J.1). They may be able to continue to exercise the company's powers, to the extent that the receiver does not wish to do so and that such exercise does not prejudice him in any way. For example, the directors, if they can find funds to do so, may pursue a claim on behalf of the company which the receiver is not interested in pursuing (*Newhart Developments Ltd v Co-operative Commercial Bank Ltd* [1978] QB 814). The directors may also, if they have funds available to them, take steps to put the company into liquidation where they think this is advisable.

(b)   Where the receiver wishes to make arrangements with the directors, whereby they provide him with management services, he will have to be extremely careful bearing in mind his obligation to report on the conduct of the directors (see chapter 9). It would be unfortunate if the receiver were to allow the company to continue to employ a director who was later subject to a report by the receiver that, in his opinion, the director was unfit to be concerned in the management of a company. The receiver is under no obligation to pay remuneration to directors voted by the members either before or after his appointment nor is he liable to pay fees under the company's articles.

(c)   The directors are under an obligation to provide such information as the administrative receiver requires and also to attend on him at such times as are reasonable (IA s 235(2)(a) and (b)).

Restrictions on Movements of Goods

4.5   Whilst manufacturing operations can be allowed to continue within the factory, it is advisable for the receiver of a trading concern to stop all movements of goods in and out of factories or other premises immediately following his appointment, to give him the opportunity to assess the situation and to arrange for a preliminary stock check to be carried out. If there is the possibility that the receiver will wish to continue trading, the closure should be for as limited a period as possible. Deliveries can be recommenced as soon as it has been established that:

(a)   the stock check is complete;
(b)   the customers to whom deliveries are to be made have no claims against the company and they are themselves creditworthy (see paragraph 5.28 below);
(c)   reservation of title claims would not make delivery of affected goods disadvantageous (see paragraph 5.29 below); and
(d)   there is an adequate system of control.

Commitments

4.6   All senior members of the staff should be instructed upon the change in emphasis which must be borne in mind in conducting the business. They should be told that they must not enter into any commitments without the consent of the receiver. Any commitments which the staff enter into without the sanction of the receiver, but which are within any ostensible authority he has conferred upon them, may be binding on him and he may become personally liable.

4.7   The receiver should take charge of the company seal, all cheque books and all company credit cards.

Banking and Cash Flow

4.8   As soon as he is appointed, the receiver should notify the company's bank (at the branch(es) where the company's account(s) are kept) of his appointment by telephone and confirm such notification by letter (appendix J.5). Similarly, he should notify any other parties who are likely to be in receipt of monies on behalf of the company. The exact time of such notification should be recorded since it could be of significance in determining the rights of set-off that the bank or other such parties might have. The receiver must also arrange for the banking account of the company to be closed and for a new account to be opened. He must instruct the company's bank to transfer the balance standing to the credit of the company, if any, to the new account.

4.9   Where the company operates a National Giro account the receiver should not continue to operate the same account after his appointment, because any amount overdrawn by or overpaid to the company prior to the appointment could be set off against any deposits made by the receiver into that account. A new receivership account should be opened with the National Giro if required.

4.10   It is common, at the start of a receivership, for a receiver to be faced with an acute cash problem as the company's own resources will, in all probability, have been drained in the period prior to the appointment of a receiver. He must therefore immediately, in consultation with the company's officials, prepare a cash flow forecast to see whether further borrowing (from outside sources) will be required. For this purpose, it will be necessary to compile a list of urgent payments.

4.11   The first payments to be made by a receiver are normally wages and salaries and those due on his appointment are usually either preferential claims or constitute essential expenses. If, however, there is the possibility that there is an insufficiency of assets charged by the floating charge to cover the preferential creditors (and these may be substantial), the receiver must be extremely careful in making any payments out of the assets in his hands.

4.12 If further borrowing has to be arranged, and the company's bankers are also the debenture holders, it is probable that the receiver will turn to them. In cases where the bankers are not the debenture holders, he may well have to go elsewhere but, in either case, security will probably have to be given. In summary:

(a) The debenture should be examined to ascertain whether the receiver has the power, for the purpose of carrying on the business of the company, to raise money on the property charged, in priority to the debentures.

(b) The receiver must obtain the consent of the debenture holders to charge the company's assets in priority to the debentures.

(c) Where a bank is the debenture holder, it will normally grant temporary overdraft facilities.

(d) Any new charge must be registered to prevent it being declared void should a liquidator be appointed.

(e) At no time should the receiver incur indebtedness to his bankers which he is not confident of repaying from future cash flow.

Company Search

4.13 Arrangements should be made for a search to be carried out of the company's file at Companies House.

Insurance

4.14 The administrative receiver should take the following action:

(a) He should notify the company's brokers or insurers of his appointment and ensure that the company's insurance policies are endorsed accordingly.

(b) He should review all the current insurance policies of the company and establish that cover is adequate and effective.

(c) He should discontinue the relevant insurance covers and obtain any refund of premiums when disposals are made, or when the business is terminated.

In considering the third party cover, if any, provided by the policies the receiver must bear in mind that the sale of goods can give rise to substantial claims for product liability being made upon the assets and possibly upon him personally if the sales were made after liquidation. The receiver should not despatch any goods prior to ascertaining the extent of third party cover (see paragraph 5.20 below).

If blanket policies have been arranged to ensure that the administrative receiver has effective insurance cover from the time of his appointment the broker should be notified (see appendix J.7).

Mail

4.15 The receiver should give instructions that he is to see all incoming and all outgoing mail. His representative should consider signing all outgoing mail if practicable.

4.16 All documents bearing the company's name leaving the company's premises must contain a statement that a receiver has been appointed. (IA s 39(1)).

Schedules of Assets

4.17 The receiver will require details of all the assets under his control and should, as soon as possible, arrange for the preparation of schedules showing, where applicable, which assets are subject to reservation of title clauses, hire purchase contracts, charges or garnishees. In most cases the receiver will also instruct agents to provide an inventory and valuation of all fixed assets and stocks (see appendix J.8). The gathering of the necessary information will take time and it is therefore necessary that instructions are given early.

4.18 The particular information to be gathered is considered in detail in chapter 6.

Informing Employees

4.19 As soon as possible after his appointment, and preferably before close of business on the first day, the receiver should talk to the employees, or if this is impractical, their elected representatives. As well as informing them of his appointment, he should explain the reasons for it, and its effect on their employment (IA s 44). He will probably not be in a position at this stage to give any information regarding their immediate prospects as this will be dependent upon the results of his examination of the business, but he should assure them that they will be kept informed of developments. A frank and open disclosure at this stage can help to stop rumours before they can cause serious problems.

4.20 Any recognised trade unions should be contacted by telephone and their representatives invited to discuss the position of their members. It is prudent at this stage to send to trade unions and the Department of Employment notices of impending redundancies and possible transfer of undertaking, even though neither may at that moment be more than a tentative possibility (see appendix H.15).

4.21 Should the procedure suggested in paragraph 4.19 above fail in its intentions, or should there have been serious discontent before the receiver's appointment, he may not obtain the co-operation of the employees. In such circumstances, he should bring to their attention that their actions can only sabotage any efforts he might be able to make to preserve the business and thus their employment. As a matter of law they could also be held liable for general rates on the premises if a 'sit in' were to occur (*Re Briant Colour Printing Co Ltd (in liquidation)* [1977] 3 All ER 968).

4.22 If the receiver's efforts do not dissuade the employees from taking an unco-operative stance, he should make whatever arrangements are necessary for the safeguarding of the assets under his control, and, where possible, disclaim responsibility for costs attaching to the occupation of the company's premises.

The Employees' Legal Position

4.23 The appointment of a receiver does not automatically terminate the employment of the company's employees unless, in a particular case, the continuance of their employment is inconsistent with the receivership (*Re Mack Trucks (Britain) Ltd* [1967] 1 WLR 780 and *Griffiths v Secretary of State for Social Services* [1974] QB 468).

4.24 The receiver, during the first fourteen days of his appointment, will have had to decide which of the company's employees he will require if he intends to carry on trading. Insofar as there will be employees retained after fourteen days, before that time has expired he will have had to write to them to explain that he is not adopting their contracts but is arranging for funds to be made available to pay their remuneration. This point has been discussed in paragraph 3.20 above.

4.25 If the receiver finds it essential to change any of the contracts of employment, to re-engage employees or to engage new employees, he should always do so as agent for the company and on the basis that his personal liability is expressly excluded (see *Re Mack Trucks* above).

4.26 The appointment of the receiver, or even his personally entering into fresh contracts of employment with the employees, does not by itself constitute a break in the continuity of employment for the purpose of calculating the redundancy payments to be met out of the Redundancy Fund.

Impending Redundancies

4.27 As mentioned in paragraph 4.20 above, it is a statutory requirement in most cases for the employer to give notice of impending redundancies to any recognised trade union and the Secretary of State for Employment (see appendix H.15). Failure to comply with the statutory requirements may lead to the receiver incurring personal liability for protective awards, if this failure occurs after liquidation (EPA ss 99-107). In addition, in selecting employees for redundancy, the receiver must ensure that there is no unfair selection which could give rise to a claim of unfair dismissal against him.

4.28 The receiver should, in addition to his statutory duties of notification, keep employees' representatives and union officials advised on matters affecting employees. The time required to be spent on this aspect should not be underestimated, especially where the workforce is large and the reorganisation plans involve a mixture of reallocation and redundancy.

4.29 Provision is made for guaranteed payments out of the Redundancy Fund in respect of certain claims made by staff, subject to stated limitations (EPCA ss 121-127). The receiver will process those claims as agent for the Secretary of State. The principal claims concerned are for accrued pay, accrued holiday pay, money in lieu of notice, basic awards of compensation for unfair dismissal, and occupational pension scheme contributions. Payment will be made out of the Redundancy Fund for the amounts outstanding on the date of the receiver's appointment, but only after the employee has been dismissed. The employees' rights under the insolvency provisions are supplemental to any rights the employees may have as preferential creditors. However, to the extent that the employees' claims are paid from the Redundancy Fund, the employees' rights will pass by subrogation to the Secretary of State (see appendix F).

4.30 As soon as possible after appointment, the receiver should arrange for a schedule of the relevant claims of employees to be prepared, distinguishing between preferential and non-preferential claims. The employees' application forms under the scheme provisions should be distributed to the company's staff as soon as possible, and dealt with in accordance with the procedures detailed in the Department of Employment's booklet 'Operational Guidance for Liquidators, Trustees, Receivers and Managers, and the Official Receiver'. If the company has an occupational pension scheme, it will be necessary for discussions to take place between the receiver and the pension scheme administrators and trustees, before any claim can be considered.

4.31 Staff who have been continuously employed by the company for a period exceeding two years are entitled to receive payment under the redundancy provisions of EPCA. In practice, the receiver should notify the local office of the Department concerned, and ensure that the company's wages records are available for inspection by the Department officials. Payments will be made up to the maximum limit laid down to the employees under the 'Guaranteed Payments Scheme' by the Department, which will then claim as an unsecured creditor.

The Transfer of Undertakings (Protection of Employment) Regulations 1981

4.32 These regulations require an employer to consult with the representatives of any trade union recognised by him, before any transfer of a business is effected (see appendix J.12). This requirement applies to all businesses irrespective of the number of employees. Failure to comply can result in an award by an industrial tribunal, to each affected employee, of compensation of up to two weeks' pay. (Such compensation can be mitigated against any protective awards or damages in lieu of notice.)

4.33 The transfer of a business acts generally as an automatic transfer to the new owner of all existing contracts of employment. The exception to this rule is the transfer of a business by a receiver or liquidator to a wholly owned subsidiary (see paragraphs 6.26 to 6.46 below). In such cases, the transfer, for the purposes of these regulations, is deemed to take place immediately before the transfer of the subsidiary or the business itself to a third party.

4.34 Where an employer dismisses his employees at any time before transferring the business to new owners who thereupon re-engage them, employment is deemed to have terminated (*Secretary of State v Spence*, The Times 2 June 1986).

4.35 Any employee dismissed immediately prior to the sale, unless the dismissal is not 'connected' with the sale or for 'economic, technical or organisational reasons', is deemed to have been unfairly dismissed.

4.36 For the purposes of these regulations, 'employees' include directors and persons employed by the company at other locations but for the purpose of the business being transferred. Pension rights are not automatically transferred.

Chapter 5

The Administration of the Receivership

5.1 The receiver should set a high standard of administrative efficiency in conducting the affairs of the company. It is his responsibility to ensure that all correspondence and other communications are handled promptly. Whenever possible, a definite decision should be made. It is important to create a feeling of confidence in suppliers, customers, and the labour force, which is essential to maintaining or improving the goodwill of the business.

5.2 The previous chapter deals with the immediate steps a receiver must take on his appointment. The present chapter covers the less immediate considerations and actions necessary for the proper administration of the receivership.

Controlling the Business

5.3 The receiver should introduce an adequate administrative system so as to exercise effective control of the business. He should institute a system of reporting so that all important matters are brought immediately to his notice.

5.4 Books of account should be completely written up and balanced to the date of the receiver's appointment, in order that the state of affairs can be ascertained at that time. The receiver is deemed to be the agent of the company and his transactions will be carried out in the name of the company (IA s 44(1)(a)). The records of the company will therefore continue unchanged. New ledger accounts, however, should be opened in the personal ledgers although there is no legal requirement to do so. This is particularly important with regard to suppliers, as it will enable the company's liabilities at the date of the appointment of the receiver to be distinguished from the receivership liabilities. It is also helpful to open new accounts in the sales ledger so that a separate control account for the receiver's transactions can be maintained (see appendix K.3).

5.5 The company's officials should continue to maintain the company's cash book, and a separate cash book must be kept by the receiver under the personal control of his own staff. Control of cash and other incoming monies, together with the receivership cheque book, should be in the hands of the receiver's own staff unless he is absolutely satisfied that the company's own system of internal control provides adequate protection.

5.6 In addition to his duty to prepare abstracts of his receipts and payments (see paragraph 10.4 below), the receiver has a duty, as the company's agent, to keep sufficient accounting records to enable the company to comply with the provisions of the Companies Act 1985 (CA 85) Sections 221-3 (*Smith Ltd v Middleton* [1979] 3 All ER 942), i.e. sufficient to disclose with reasonable accuracy, at any time, the financial position of the company at that time.

Reporting to the Bank

5.7 The first meeting between the bank and the receiver, at the time of his appointment, is of vital importance because, at this meeting, if not before, all the major areas of difficulty known to the bank can be reviewed.

5.8   At that same meeting, the receiver should agree with the bank what reports it wishes to receive, including their contents and frequency. As a general practice, the receiver should submit, as soon as he has sufficient information, his first forecasts of the way the receivership is likely to develop and of its ultimate outcome. Subsequently, he should update the position at quarterly intervals, and, in the early stages, at more frequent intervals, if the receivership is likely to be a long one.

5.9   Quite apart from these regular updating reports, the bank will welcome an overall review about two months before the end of its own financial half year, to tie in with the bank's own bad and doubtful debts review.

5.10 The basis on which the receiver will be charging his fees will normally need to be discussed with the bank at an early stage. At this juncture, the receiver should also give the bank some indication of the numbers of staff that he will have to deploy, and of the way in which he expects costs to arise.

5.11 In addition to financial reports, the bank will also expect to be given warning of major events as they occur. As far as asset realisations are concerned, it should be told, as soon as possible, of any variations from original forecasts, with suitable explanations.

5.12 Reports should be as concise and factual as possible; a bank is not interested in long-winded commentaries.

Contracts

5.13 All contracts should be reviewed by the receiver so that he can ascertain whether the amount of money required for their completion will be more or less than the net proceeds arising upon the completion. A statement should be prepared showing the extent to which the work has been performed or cost incurred and the amount outstanding with particular regard to:

(a)   the value of work performed;
(b)   the amount of work outstanding;
(c)   the monies paid to date and the amount still due under the contract;
(d)   the accrued liability to nominated sub-contractors who can be paid direct by the employing authority (see paragraph 8.19 below); and
(e)   whether performance bonds have been given by the debenture holders and are secured under the debenture;

and in the case of construction contracts:

(f)   the value of materials on site not included in the value of work performed; and
(g)   the value of plant on site which may be retained by the employing authority if the contract is terminated.

5.14 The receiver must also consider the effect upon continuance of any contract of the following:

(a)   Possible loss of specialist personnel.
(b)   Problems of continuance of supply.
(c)   Whether claims from any customer are outstanding on the contract or any other contract. In the case of a contract with a Government department, it will be necessary to consider possible claims from other Government departments, whether arising under contract or not (*Re D H Curtis (Builders) Ltd* [1978] 2 WLR 28) (see paragraph 5.60 below).
(d)   The length of time the contract will take to complete.
(e)   The effect of variations (if any) to the original contract.
(f)   Whether the employing authority has the power to terminate the contract upon the appointment of the receiver.
(g)   If the contract gives no power to terminate as in (f) above, whether the contract can be terminated on the appointment of a liquidator. (This is relevant because

the receiver may decide to continue the contract only for it to be terminated by the employing authority at a later date.)

5.15 It may be necessary to negotiate with creditors who, as sub-contractors, have work partly completed, in order to ascertain the terms on which they are prepared to continue with the contract. Creditors in such circumstances are often favourably placed. They are in a position to refuse to complete a contract unless they are paid not only for the work carried out after the appointment of the receiver, but also the amounts already due, for which they would otherwise rank only as unsecured creditors.

5.16 The overriding consideration is to obtain the maximum cash benefit and the administrative receiver is free to cause the company to repudiate or ignore its outstanding contractual obligations to third parties if he so chooses (*Airlines Airspares Ltd v Handley Page Ltd and another* [1970] 2 WLR 163). He should discard all unprofitable contracts as a matter of course and must ensure that none of his actions constitutes adoption of the contract in whole or in part.

Customers' Goods

5.17 Goods in the possession of the company may already belong to customers. The point at which title in goods passes from the company to a customer is determined by the terms of the contract of sale and, in the absence of any express provisions in such terms, by a number of legal rules set out in the Sale of Goods Act 1979. Broadly, the rules state that, where goods are specific and in a deliverable state, title passes when the contract is made. If, however, the seller is bound to do something to the goods, either to put them into a deliverable state, or to ascertain the price (e.g. to weigh or measure them), title may not pass until such act has been completed and notified to the buyer. Where goods are supplied on approval or a sale or return basis, title does not pass until acceptance is notified or on the expiration of any fixed term, or reasonable time, without notification of rejection. In the case of unascertained goods, title passes when goods are appropriated to the contract or delivered. It should be noted that the payment of a deposit does not establish title.

5.18 The question is of considerable importance to a receiver, since if title has already passed to the customer, then the customer can claim the particular goods concerned. If title has not passed, the receiver will usually be able to insist on being paid under a new contract before making delivery, and the customer will be left with a claim for damages against the company. As the contract was entered into before the receiver was appointed, these damages will normally rank only as unsecured claims. Where title has passed to a customer, the goods should be treated in the same way as other third-party property (see paragraph 5.82 below).

Warranties on Goods Sold

5.19 A receiver should consider whether the circumstances are such that, in addition to any general disclaimer of personal liability, he should indicate on all invoices for goods sold that he will not be personally responsible for warranties on goods sold, and that goods are sold under those conditions. Ideally he should agree terms of trading with each customer prior to supplying any goods to that customer.

5.20 Neither the company nor the receiver is able to contract out of liability for negligence which causes death or personal injury. Liability for negligence which causes other types of loss can only be avoided by exemption clauses which satisfy the requirements of reasonableness. The company will also be unable to contract out of liability for breach of certain warranties where the goods sold are of a type ordinarily bought for private use or consumption and are sold to a person who is not buying them in the course of his business. In respect of other sales made by the company any exclusion clauses may be unenforceable if it can be shown that it would not be fair or reasonable to allow reliance on them (Supply of Goods (Implied Terms) Act 1973 and Unfair Contract Terms Act 1977).

5.21 In the case of some types of business, the sale of the company's goods can involve the risk of uninsurable liabilities in contract or tort. If the receiver carries on and sells goods without excluding personal liability, then he could be personally liable and such liabilities could remain outstanding for a number of years. Even if he seeks to exclude personal liability, there must be a doubt as to whether he will be able to do so in all circumstances. The receiver may seek to protect himself by transferring the business to a wholly owned subsidiary formed specially for the purpose. (See paragraph 6.26 below.)

The Financial Services Act 1986

5.22 The administrative receiver does not have specific exemption from registration under the Act. However, if the company carries on a business requiring registration and it has duly registered then the administrative receiver is protected by the Law of Agency. He will not be carrying on the business as principal but as agent. He must ensure however that the rules applicable to the business before his appointment continue to be observed in the conduct of such of his activities as constitute investment business. This situation is not altered by the company going into liquidation.

The Data Protection Act 1984

5.23 The administrative receiver must be aware of the fact that if the company retains electronically processed personnel information it will have been necessary for the company to have registered under the above Act. The administrative receiver himself, if utilising this information in any way as is likely, will have to ensure that he is registered personally.

The Consumer Credit Act 1974

5.24 If goods are to be supplied to individuals, sole traders, or partnerships on credit terms which include the charging of interest, the company or receiver must possess the appropriate licence under the Consumer Credit Act 1974. It is a criminal offence to engage in activities which are controlled by the Act without the required licence. A receiver and manager appointed in relation to property of a body corporate will generally be an agent of the body corporate (see paragraph 3.20 above) and, as such, he will be covered by the company's licence should he choose to continue the business for any reason. If the company does not already hold a licence, or if a licence in the name of the company has expired, the receiver and manager will need to take out a licence or to renew it in the name of the company. To decide whether to take out a licence in his own name or to renew it in the name of the company, and to ascertain the procedures, reference must be made to the relevant sections of the Act and to any subsequent Regulations. Any doubts must be cleared with the Office of Fair Trading.

Whilst a receiver and manager will generally be the agent of a body corporate, there may be an element of doubt in certain circumstances where, for example, he is the agent of the debenture holders. There can also exist the situation where he is appointed in relation to a part of the property of a licensee and where he carries on a part of the business. All practising chartered accountants are covered by a group licence.

Public Services

5.25 Notwithstanding the fact that the suppliers of public services may be creditors of the company, the receiver can request supplies of gas, electricity, water and telecommunication services as from the date of his appointment. The supplier may ask for his personal guarantee for any charges in respect of that supply but cannot, as a condition of providing that supply, demand payment for any amounts outstanding at the date of the appointment (IA s 233).

General Rates

5.26 Insofar as general rates are outstanding at the appointment of a receiver, as the receiver is agent of the company, the company is liable for any rates. Following *Ratford and Hayward v Northavon District Council* (The Times 24 May 1986) the appointment of an administrative receiver does not constitute a change of occupation, and until the company goes into liquidation the receiver has no liability for rates. The position, once the company has gone into liquidation, is not completely clear but it is considered that the loss of the administrative receiver's agency while he is in possession of the premises is a 'change of occupation' enabling the local authority to apportion rates and seek those relating to the post liquidation period directly from the receiver.

5.27 The local authority may attempt to levy distress after the receiver's appointment. There is a lack of authority on this point and legal advice should be sought.

Suppliers

5.28 Notwithstanding the fact that the receiver has an obligation to send a copy of the notice advertising his appointment to all creditors (see paragraph 9.4 below), he should write to all suppliers as soon as possible not only notifying them of his appointment but also informing them that no goods should be supplied to the business except against orders signed by the receiver or his authorised representative (see appendix J.10). He should also include his terms of trade. Similar instructions must be given to the staff, and the receiver should ensure that these instructions reach everyone in the company's employ who is at any time likely to accept delivery of goods (sec appendix K.5). The receiver may incur losses by becoming liable to pay for goods originally ordered by the company for a contract which he decides to abandon.

Retention of Title

5.29 It should not be assumed that the retention or acceptance of goods necessarily implies that the receiver is liable to pay for them out of the funds coming into his hands. The position is as follows:

(a) If the contract for the supply of the goods has been made by the company before the receiver's appointment, and under that contract title to the goods has already passed to the company, the receiver will be entitled to such goods on behalf of the company, and at the same time will not be obliged to pay for them.

(b) On the other hand, if title to the goods has not passed to the company, or only passes to the company on payment, then the receiver, if he does not wish to use the goods, should not pay for them but should allow the supplier to collect them.

(c) A condition of sale postponing the passing of title in goods is commonly known as a 'reservation of title' clause. Such provisions in a sale contract are often called 'Romalpa clauses' after the English case that first brought them to prominence (*Aluminium Industrie Vaassen B V v Romalpa Aluminium Ltd* [1976] 1 WLR 676). This case concerned a sale made under a clause reserving title in the goods until any debts due by the company to the supplier had been paid. It was held by the Court of Appeal that the reservation clause was effective in that particular contract.

Statutory Provisions

5.30 Section 17 of the Sale of Goods Act 1979 provides that ownership of goods shall be transferred from the seller to the buyer at such time as they intend and that their intention shall be ascertained by reference to the contract terms, their conduct 'and the circumstances of the case'. The parties are therefore able to agree that title shall pass upon payment of the invoice or, in England and Wales, upon payment of all amounts due to the supplier. If there is no evidence as to the time at which the parties intended title to be transferred, Section 18 sets out a number of rules for deciding when the transfer is effective, none of which is dependent on payment. Reservation of title must therefore be specified in the contract if it is to be effective.

What are the Terms of the Contract?

5.31 When considering a reservation of title claim, it will be necessary to identify the point in time at which a binding contract came into existence between the parties. Commonsense would say that if a customer orders some goods and receives confirmation that the order has been accepted by the supplier a binding contract comes into existence at that point. That will not necessarily be the case, however.

5.32 Under English law there must be both an offer and an acceptance of that offer for a contract to be formed. But the offer must be accepted as it stands; a purported acceptance which introduces some new or different term is simply a counter-offer which the original offeror is free to accept or reject as he wishes (*Brogden v Metropolitan Railway Company* [1877] 2 App Cas 666).

5.33 For example, an order for '2,000 Mk III plugs for delivery 30 June' is an offer to enter into a contract to purchase 2,000 plugs provided they are delivered on 30 June. A reply that says 'We confirm we will deliver 2,000 Mk III plugs on 1 July' is not an acceptance of that offer but a counter-offer; a different date has been proposed. There will be no binding contract unless and until there is some evidence that the parties are in agreement as to the date. It is possible that no contract will come into existence until the goods have been delivered and accepted by the original offeror.

5.34 Difficulties can arise when a customer orders goods using its own order form bearing one set of conditions and the supplier acknowledges the order on its own form containing a different set of conditions. In theory there is no binding contract; the customer has offered to buy goods on its conditions and the supplier has made a counter-offer to sell on its conditions instead. In normal circumstances the goods will be delivered and the customer will pay for them without either party having to worry about identifying the precise terms of the contract. Once the purchaser becomes insolvent these normal circumstances no longer apply.

5.35 If the chain of the exchange of documents with contradictory terms continues, the set of terms that will apply to the contract will normally be the last set provided by one party to the other *before the delivery of the goods* (or the first delivery, if more than one). Conditions could be contained in:

(a)   the delivery note (if handed over before the goods are physically accepted);
(b)   the invoice (if received before the goods);
(c)   an acknowledgement of the order;
(d)   the order itself;
(e)   a quotation;
(f)   a trade catalogue or price list;
(g)   a set of standard conditions delivered by one party to the other; or
(h)   a letter.

5.36 However, once one party does something that can be construed as an unconditional acceptance of the offer made by the other a binding contract will come into existence at that point and the fact that subsequent documents contain an inconsistent set of conditions will be irrelevant unless the parties specifically agree to change the terms of the contract (*Chapleton v Barry Urban District Council* [1940] 1 KB 532). If, for example, the suppliers' sales manager receives a written order and accepts it over the telephone any conditions contained on the order form will apply even though the written acknowledgement of the order may refer to different conditions.

5.37 If the only conditions are contained on the back of the supplier's invoices, the receipt of the first such invoice may be sufficient to bring those conditions to the attention of the buyer, who in the absence of any evidence or dealings to the contrary will then be bound by them in his subsequent transactions with the supplier (*Spurling v Bradshaw* [1956] 2 All ER 121). Nevertheless, it is generally accepted that a purchaser cannot be expected to read every set of conditions on every document issued by a supplier to see whether they have been changed. A change in standard conditions will only apply if they have been brought to the other party's attention.

5.38 It will usually be sufficient for a document to refer to standard conditions that are available on request or common to the industry. The other party is then on notice that the offer is subject to conditions and it is up to him to find out what those conditions are if he does not know already.

5.39 If the supplier's conditions were written in a foreign language not understood by those acting on the company's behalf, and no translation was provided, legal advice should be taken as to whether or not they are binding on the company in the particular circumstances. In the Scottish case of *Armour v Thyssen Edelstahlwerke AG* [1986] SLT 273, the conditions were in German but both parties acknowledged that they applied to the contract. However it must be remembered that the law in Scotland differs to that in England and Wales.

What Law Applies?

5.40 The ownership of goods must be determined according to the law of the place where the goods are situated and not according to the law governing the contract or even the law of the place where the goods were situated at the time the contract was executed (*Emerald Stainless Steel Ltd v South Side Distribution Ltd* [1983] SLT 162, another Scottish case).

5.41 Nevertheless, it is suggested that advice be taken from a lawyer in the country concerned in all cases where the contract itself is expressed to be subject to foreign law and the amounts at stake are material. It is at least arguable that title cannot have been reserved if it is impossible to do so under the law under which the contract was made. Italian law, for example, does not recognise reservation of title.

Is the Reservation of Title Legally Effective?

5.42 In the case of an English company, unless the clause reserves *legal* ownership it must be registered as a charge under Section 395 of the Companies Act 1985 (*Re Bond Worth Ltd* [1980] Ch 228; Section 395 does not apply to Scotland).

5.43 An extension of the reservation of title to any manufactured items into which the supplier's goods are incorporated should similarly be registered as a charge (*Re Peachdart Ltd* [1984] Ch 131). It is considered that an extension to the proceeds of sale should also be registered as a charge *unless* it is provided that the company acts as the supplier's agent on any sale and the goods are sold in the state in which they were received from the supplier. The fact that a purported reservation of title to items manufactured by the customer or to the proceeds of sale is void as an unregistered charge will not necessarily invalidate the reservation of title to the goods themselves (*Clough Mill Ltd v Martin* [1984] 128 SJ 850).

5.44 In Scotland, title can only be reserved pending payment for the goods themselves. A clause which purports to reserve title pending payment of *all* sums due to the supplier will be void as an attempt to create a charge over movables without possession (*Deutz Engines Ltd v Terex Ltd* [1984] SLT 273).

Has Title been Transferred?

5.45 If title passes on payment for the goods themselves, ownership will be transferred on payment of the invoice.

5.46 If title passes on payment of all sums due to the supplier, ownership will be transferred upon settlement of the supplier's account at a particular date even if he becomes a creditor again. (But note that such a reservation is not valid in Scotland in any event. See paragraph 5.44 above.)

5.47 A clause which specifies that title passes on payment of all sums due to the supplier 'and its associated companies' will normally be void for uncertainty. The customer is not expected to know the identity of all the supplier's associates.

5.48 Title will pass to the customer as soon as the items concerned lose their identity (*Borden (UK) Ltd v Scottish Timber Products Ltd and another* [1981] Ch 25). For example, rubber will lose its identity when converted into tyres and a piece of equipment will lose its identity if it becomes a fixture and therefore part of the freehold.

Is There Any Stock On Hand?

5.49 No supplier will be able to claim reservation of title to goods unless he can show that the company holds items originally supplied by him. Assuming that he does have a valid reservation of title, however, it is not clear whether once he has identified goods that he supplied the onus is on him to prove that he has not been paid for those particular goods (or that they were supplied since his account was last settled in full, as the case may be) or on the company to prove that it *has* paid for them.

5.50 Each supplier must be able to identify his own goods. If there are a number of creditors supplying identical items, it is not sufficient for them to show that goods in stock must have been supplied by one or the other of them.

5.51 The supplier is entitled to rely on the evidence of the company's records and employees as well as his own.

Dealing with Reservation of Title Claims

5.52 A supplier claiming reservation of title should be asked to send a representative to the company's premises in order to establish of exactly what stocks, if any, he claims to be owner. He should also be asked to complete a questionnaire in the form of appendix G. The receiver's files should include a schedule of all assets subject to retention of title claims.

5.53 The supplier will only be able to claim VAT bad debt relief to the extent that he abandons any claim to the goods themselves. Even if there are identified stocks over which a supplier has an effective reservation of title, it should be remembered that it may still be possible to negotiate a purchase of the goods from him for less than normal cost as in many cases the supplier will prefer cash to the goods. The receiver however has the choice of releasing the goods which he should do if he has no use for them.

Generally

5.54 Reservation of title can, of course, apply to plant and machinery as well as goods for resale or manufacture.

Avoidance of Counter Claims

5.55 The receiver should ensure that goods are not despatched to any person who may be a creditor of the company, until the creditor agrees to make payment in cash in respect of supplies made by the receiver. Procedures should therefore be introduced to enable the staff and the despatch department to know the names of persons who are likely to have counter-claims against the company. Where counter-claims exist, either cash should be obtained in advance or an undertaking not to claim set-off obtained (see appendix J.20) before the goods are despatched. An undertaking should not be accepted if there is doubt concerning the creditworthiness of the customer. (See also paragraph 5.56 et seq below.)

Set-off

5.56 There will sometimes be ordinary creditors who have a right of set-off and the receiver must accept this right if, for instance, the company has supplied goods to a customer to whom the company is indebted. The fundamental conditions with regard to set-off are that:

(a)   there is mutuality between the two transactions concerned, e.g. money due to a trustee cannot be set off against money due from him personally, and

(b)   the right to set-off must have arisen prior to the appointment of the receiver.

5.57 Rights of set-off also arise where, as a result of trading by the receiver, both debits and credits arise between him and some other person. It has never been authoritatively decided whether a third party can set off debts due by him to the receiver, incurred after the receivership, against liabilities of the company to the third party incurred before the receivership. If, however, the third party was aware of the crystallisation of the floating charge, it is suggested that, in principle, there should not be a right of set-off in these circumstances unless the debits and credits arise out of fulfilment of the same contract. Generally, a sum becoming due after the appointment of a receiver to the company under a new contract with him cannot be set off against the sum due by the company before the appointment. However, there could be a valid set-off if the sum becoming due to the company after the appointment arises under any pre-existing arrangement continued by the receiver (*Rother Iron Works Ltd v Canterbury Precision Engineering Ltd* [1973] 1 All ER 394). This principle has been extended to a carrier's lien arising after the appointment, but under an agreement entered into before the appointment (*George Barker (Transport) Ltd v Eynon* [1974] 1 WLR 462). Rights of set-off raise very difficult problems and it is suggested that legal advice should always be taken when there is any doubt over claims made.

5.58 The receiver must always consider the possibility of other persons having a right of set-off before deliveries are made to them, or before they are entrusted with the company's assets or documents of title. Receivers must therefore take particular care before deciding to continue with Government contracts. The Crown has the right to set off debits and credits even if these did not arise from contracts (*Re D H Curtis (Builders) Ltd* [1978] 2 WLR 28). The Crown Proceedings Act 1947 provides, however, that the Crown, when sued in the name of a Government department, should not, without leave of the Court, avail itself of any set-off if the subject matter did not relate to that department. It is considered that the Crown will always be given leave to set-off debts due to and from different departments as against a company in receivership. One important aspect which needs to be watched is VAT. If the company continues to trade, and VAT is likely to be reclaimable in respect of post-receivership trading, H M Customs and Excise will not refund that VAT as long as there exists a pre-receivership liability (unless the refund arises on a Form VAT 427). This approach by H M Customs and Excise is based on its interpretation of the VAT regulations and not on any right of set-off. At the time of writing a test case is being brought to clarify the position where such situations arise.

5.59 In *Re Unit 2 Windows Ltd* [1985] 2 All ER 647 it was held that amounts to be set-off should be applied against preferential and non-preferential claims pro rata. Where the Crown is claiming set-off, therefore, the total amounts due from all Government departments should be set pro rata against the amounts due to all Government departments. Arguably, amounts due to and from the same Government department should be set against each other and only the balance set against sums due to and from other Government departments. The counter argument is that, since 'the Crown is indivisible', the identity of the particular department concerned is irrelevant and that all debits should be set against all credits unless they relate to the same contract or account. Legal advice should be sought should a dispute arise in a material case. Set-off cannot be applied against employee claims subrogated to the Department of Employment under the Employment Protection (Consolidation) Act 1978. These do not constitute Crown claims at the relevant date. Legal advice should be sought if material sums are due from a health authority. Health authorities also act as agents for the Department of Health and Social Security and sums due from them are therefore Crown debts (*R A Cullen Ltd v Nottingham Health Authority*, The Times 1 August 1986).

5.60 Another point when considering the position regarding Crown set-off arises if claims can be instituted by a Government department as a result of the cessation of trade (e.g. clawback of regional development grants). Even though agreement may be reached with Government departments to disregard Crown set-off, it must be remembered that their attitude might change on the appointment of a liquidator.

Debtors

5.61 The receiver must write to all debtors informing them of his appointment, and requesting payment of monies due to the company (see appendix J.23).

5.62 The receiver should examine the terms under which goods have been sold, to see if there are alternative routes to recovery in the event that he is unable to obtain payment from the debtor (e.g. reservation of title clauses).

5.63 Where there are large numbers of debts payable by instalments, the receiver may also consider the alternative of selling the outstanding debts for a fixed sum to a collecting agency.

5.64 It has become increasingly common for companies to discount or factor their debts, particularly those companies with liquidity problems. Agreements for discounting or factoring take several forms but by far the most common arrangement is for the company to enter into a 'block discounting' agreement with a finance house. The finance house buys the debts for say 75% or 80% of their book value, normally with the right of equitable assignment to itself of all subsequent debts discounted under the main agreement (*Olds Discount Co Ltd v John Playfair Ltd* [1938] 3 All ER 275). The agreements of most finance houses have been drafted to ensure that the equitable assignment is good. Legal advice should, however, be taken on the validity of the assignment, since there is always the possibility that the assignment might be invalid as an unregistered charge on book debts.

5.65 The receiver will probably find that, despite the equitable assignment, there are provisions under the agreement for monies collected, in excess of the price paid (less commission charges and costs of collection) to be paid to the company. The receiver need take no action other than to obtain a periodical report if collections are made by the finance house, or if he is advised that the equitable assignment of the debts is good in law. Any surplus payable to the company will probably not be received for some considerable time.

5.66 Where collections are being made by the company and the receiver is satisfied that the assignments are good in law, he must consider whether there is likely to be any eventual surplus available for the debenture holder or creditors, and:

(a) If no surplus is likely, he should discontinue collection and allow the finance house to collect the debts.
(b) If it is confidently expected there will be an eventual surplus after payment of all costs, the best course for the receiver is to continue to collect the debts, with the finance house meeting the costs of collection on a week-to-week basis. These costs will be added to the finance house's security and recovered by them before any surplus is released to the receiver. By continuing the collection procedure, the receiver retains some measure of control.
(c) In the event of any surplus funds not being required to satisfy the debenture, the receiver should still ensure that any arrangements he makes do not prejudice the rights of the principals concerned.

Pension Schemes

5.67 Occupational pension schemes are frequently encountered in corporate receiverships. In theory, the administrative receiver will not need to concern himself with these schemes further than dealing with related claims against the insolvent employer, and will be content to leave the administration to the trustees. However, a more active interest is likely to be necessary where:

(a) the insolvent employer is the administrator of the scheme or a trustee, or the trustees are unable or unwilling to act; and/or
(b) the scheme is in surplus, and the insolvent employer may be entitled to share in a distribution; or
(c) it is desirable to continue the scheme in a 'going concern'.

The degree of involvement will depend on the individual circumstances of the case, taking into account the commercial justification and moral and legal obligations. Specialist advice will often be necessary. It should be noted that whilst many schemes are managed by insurance companies, the 'managers' rarely understand the implications of the appointment of a receiver. In any event the receiver should obtain details of the pensions position as soon as possible after his appointment.

5.68 Where a business is to be sold as a going concern it will often be desirable to ensure that any employees' entitlements under a pension scheme continue to accrue up to the date of sale. If the trustees are willing and able to act, this should present no problem, apart from ensuring that any necessary employer's contributions are paid and any claims against the employer are dealt with expeditiously. However, if the trustees are unable or unwilling to act then the receiver will need to ensure that effective trustees are appointed in accordance with the formal scheme documents. Usually the employer will be able to dismiss and appoint trustees.

5.69 It should be noted that a receiver could be held personally liable for his actions or omissions where the employer itself is a trustee, particularly if it is the sole trustee. Legal advice should be sought in such circumstances.

5.70 When the business is sold, care should be taken to avoid giving warranties and indemnities regarding pensions in the sale agreement. Legal advice should be sought on any such warranties or indemnities which have to be conceded.

5.71 Where a scheme is to be wound up it is possible that there may be a refund due to the employer. This will occur when augmentation of members' benefits would:

(a) exceed the maximum approvable by the Inland Revenue; or
(b) exceed the maximum permitted under the scheme rules; or
(c) require the employer's consent and this is not given; or
(d) result in excessive benefits, in the opinion of the trustees.

This is an area that should be considered carefully by the receiver, even prior to his appointment if possible, as the realisation of a large surplus could drastically improve the financial position of the employer. Section 46 of the Finance Act 1986 has however now imposed a tax liability of 40% on any surplus returnable to the employer. This tax cannot be relieved by any set-off whatever.

5.72 As with the preservation of entitlements in a going concern, the realisation of a surplus will present fewer problems if there are trustees prepared to act. However, if the business has ceased to trade it is quite probable that there will be no effective trustees. Except for the largest schemes, the trustees will often consist of senior management with little idea of their obligations under the scheme. If the company is being wound up they may now be pursuing other interests and probably believe their trusteeship has terminated.

5.73 If large numbers of staff are leaving or are due to be dismissed, then trustees will normally be required by the trust deed to inform employees of their entitlements. Care should be taken not to treat the scheme as being wound up until all employees have had an opportunity to withdraw from the scheme, as otherwise their options may be restricted. If any amendments are required to the trust documents to achieve a fairer distribution of assets, then resort must be had to the alteration powers contained in such trust documents and the amendments duly made, provided that the alteration powers so permit. The agreement of the receiver will almost certainly be required to any such amendments and will be required if he is to execute any document on behalf of the company.

5.74 If a pension scheme is to cease to be contracted-out under the Social Security Pensions Act 1975, the Occupational Pensions Board (OPB) should be informed as soon as possible so that the relevant Certificate can be cancelled. Action must then be taken to preserve the Guaranteed Minimum Pensions under that Act. If a pension scheme was contracted-out under the National Insurance Act 1965, then Equivalent Pension Benefits must also be preserved but these are relatively insignificant.

5.75 Arrears of contributions due from the employer or deducted from employees' remuneration in respect of the twelve months immediately preceding the receiver's appointment will be payable, subject to certain limits, to the trustees by the Secretary of State for Employment (see appendix F). (EPCA s 123(5)). Priority is given to certain contributions to occupational pension schemes.

5.76 Generally an insurance company will be involved which will be able to provide much of any information required and also draft any documents that are needed. It will also be able to advise regarding the action that needs to be taken regarding the continuation of life cover; forms to the OPB regarding contracting-out; and the relevant benefits available to employees on leaving service. If there is any doubt as to how to proceed, the advice of an actuary should be sought.

Patents and Trade Marks

5.77 The receiver should ascertain the following:

(a) Whether any patents, registered designs, copyright material, know-how, or computer programs ('industrial property rights') are used under licence by the company in connection with its business. If industrial property rights are used under licence, the receiver should ensure that the terms of the licence are complied with. It is not uncommon for a licence to stipulate that on receivership or liquidation of the licensee the original user rights are suspended.

(b) Whether any of the company's activities or products are carried on or sold under licence, or are likely to infringe industrial property rights of a third party. If this is the case, and the receiver carries on such activities or sells the products, he may find himself involved in a lawsuit. In certain circumstances, the receiver may become personally liable for infringement of industrial property rights.

(c) Whether the company owns any industrial property rights which could have a value.

Agents

5.78 The receiver should take great care in dealing with agents of the company (see appendix J.24). He should make it quite clear in any dealings that he himself is acting in his capacity as an agent of the company. He may find that where non-employees have been acting as agents they might claim to be employees entitled to preferential treatment with regard to any outstanding commission due to them. This claim is unjustified, as only employees can rank preferentially for arrears of salary or commission (see appendix E).

5.79 The receiver must avoid taking personal responsibility in his dealings with an agent. The agent's terms of reference will probably be set out in an agreement between the agent and the company, and this agreement must be studied in detail. It may also be necessary to take legal advice, since precipitate termination of an agency agreement by a receiver may give rise to claims against the company. Particular care is necessary in the case of foreign agents, who may enjoy special rights under their local law.

5.80 Agents often have in their possession, or under their control, property belonging to the company that they will endeavour to retain against any monies due to them. Agents are entitled to retain and sell certain assets of the company, but before allowing an agent to take this step the receiver should review recent case law and particularly *Rolls Razor Ltd v Cox* [1967] 1 QB 552 where it was held that the agent was entitled to set off, against monies due to him, sale proceeds in his possession and the proceeds of the sale of goods held by him for sale, but not the proceeds of the sale of goods held by him for demonstration purposes. It is necessary to take legal advice in difficult cases.

Tenancies

5.81 Tenancies should be reviewed in order to see whether it is possible to obtain vacant possession with the intention to sell. There should also be a check as to whether tenants have been in any way breaching their leases. If rent is accepted when no tenancy exists or a lease is terminable because of a breach, the receiver could lose any right he might have to challenge the tenancy or terminate the lease. In the case of a breach, this will apply whenever the breach has come to the notice of either the receiver and his staff or the company. To protect himself as far as possible, the receiver should therefore write to the directors or other responsible company official (see appendix J.31). Once he has satisfied himself that a tenancy exists and the tenant is not known to be in breach, he should give notice of his appointment to each tenant with a request that all rents due are paid to him (see appendix J.32). In cases of doubt legal advice should be taken before letters are sent to the tenants.

Third-Party Property

5.82 If the company has property on its premises belonging to customers or others, they should be informed that the property is held by the company at their own risk. The customers can then remove their property or leave it at the company's premises at their own risk. Unless notice is given (see appendix J.27), the receiver may incur some personal liability if the property of a third party deteriorates whilst in his possession.

Hire Purchase

5.83 The position with regard to assets on hire purchase (see also paragraphs 5.84 et seq below) may well affect the receiver's decision as to whether or not to trade. In practice, his approach will, to a large extent, be determined by the attitude of the owner. The position is generally as follows:

(a) If the market value of the equipment exceeds the outstanding instalments, it is most likely that the owner will insist on his full rights.

(b) If the outstanding instalments exceed the market value of the equipment, the owner will generally co-operate with the receiver in the hope that a purchaser will be found.

5.84 In the circumstances as set out in paragraph 5.83(a) above, the receiver may be able to thwart an attempt by the finance company to repossess the equipment if the agreement has not been breached, and payments are up-to-date, or the asset concerned has become a fixture (see paragraph 7.9 below).

5.85 Alternatively, the receiver may be able to negotiate with the hire purchase company to retain the use of the assets subject to hire purchase upon payment of only current instalments falling due in the receivership period, and without discharging any arrears.

5.86 The receiver may decide that certain assets are not required for the purpose of trading or he may wish to realise the equity in them. The hire purchase companies generally have a consolidation clause in their standard forms of agreement. This means, in effect, that all agreements must be dealt with as one rather than taking them piecemeal, and the receiver will then have to consider the extent to which any equity in some assets may be eroded by a shortfall on others.

5.87 If a sale of the going concern has been negotiated, the receiver must satisfy the interests of the hire purchase company before assigning the assets involved. It is sometimes possible, in the course of the negotiations, to persuade the owner to settle for an amount less than the legal liability under the hire purchase agreements or to arrange for the purchaser to assume the liabilities under the hire purchase contracts.

Value Added Tax

5.88 The requirements of current legislation, particularly as regards de-registration, have to be considered. There are special provisions enabling receivers to recover certain VAT inputs after de-registration has taken place. Where the company is involved in a group registration, it will usually be advisable to cancel the group registration to avoid the company incurring liability for VAT for other members of the group (*Re Nadler Enterprises Ltd* [1981] 1 WLR 23).

Government Regulations

5.89 The receiver should instruct company officials and managers to comply with all Government regulations covering fire, building, safety, food in canteens, and general hygiene. If the officials of the company default, the receiver may well incur personal liability (see appendix K.1).

Regional Development Grants

5.90 There are two separate aspects to consider:

(a) Regional development grants may have been paid to the company prior to the appointment of the receiver, but the four-year period of qualifying manufacturing use may not have expired.

(b) Grants on assets installed by or on behalf of the company may have been claimed but not received by the company, at the date of the receiver's appointment.

5.91 The receiver, in his handling of the company's affairs, must at all times consider the effect of his actions upon the regional development grant position. The following factors should be taken into account:

(a) Where the receiver decides to close down a particular operation, certain assets may go out of qualifying manufacturing use, thus giving rise to a claim from the Department of Industry for repayment of the grant. This will be an unsecured claim against the company but can be set off by the Department against amounts due to the company. The claim for repayment will generally be reduced to a proportion of the grants paid on a time apportionment basis, but such reduction is concessionary on the part of the Department.

(b) The receiver may sell certain assets of the company before the expiry of the four-year qualifying period. This will give rise to a claim for repayment of the grant paid on such assets unless the receiver obtains undertakings from the purchaser which are acceptable to the Department. A receiver can be criticised if no attempt is made to obtain such undertakings, as a claim from the Department will increase the amount of unsecured creditors. However, if such undertakings can only be obtained on the basis of a reduction of the selling price, then it may well be in the best interests of the secured creditor that such undertakings are not insisted upon.

(c) The fact that further grants are due but not yet paid, is a factor to be taken into account by the receiver when considering whether or not to continue the trade. If he stops trading, grants due may not be paid, and claims will be received in respect of the assets taken out of qualifying use.

Assets in Scotland

5.92 The law applicable to receivers in Scotland is different from that in England and, as regards floating charges, is governed by Sections 410-424 of the Companies Act 1985. Scottish legal advice may be necessary if assets covered by a debenture issued by an English registered company are located in Scotland.

The Shareholders

5.93 The receiver is not accountable directly to the shareholders. He has no responsibilities for the maintenance of the share registers or for the payment of registrars. All statutory requirements are the responsibility of the directors and it is their duty to see that these have been properly carried out. In practice, the directors will probably have no funds available to them, and so may be unable to fulfil their responsibilities.

5.94 However, the receiver may sometimes find that it is to his advantage if the statutory records are maintained, e.g. where a reconstruction is envisaged, he will probably allow the company's staff to assist in such matters as the maintenance of the share registers.

5.95 Where a company listed on the Stock Exchange is in receivership, it is likely that the listing will have to be suspended. It is the duty of the directors, not the receiver, to make such an application to the Stock Exchange. Following suspension there will be many enquiries from shareholders. These should be referred to the directors, or to the liquidator, if one is appointed.

5.96 Statutory obligations to convene meetings and to prepare the accounts of the company continue regardless of the appointment of a receiver. These obligations fall upon the directors (see paragraph 4.4 above), though they will probably be unable to fulfil them.

Taxation during Receivership

5.97 Generally a receiver appointed out of Court is not liable to pay the tax due on profits earned, or capital gains realised, in respect of the business and assets under his control. Such tax is assessable on the company and not the receiver.

5.98 If the tax relates to a period after the company has gone into liquidation, it will be a liquidation expense. If it relates to a period before the commencement of the winding-up, it will rank as an unsecured claim.The receiver is not responsible for agreeing any corporation tax liabilities arising during the period of his appointment but he should make sufficient information available to the directors or the liquidator to enable them to do so.

5.99 It should be noted, however, that a receiver must pay to the relevant authorities taxes and duties collected or deducted by him in the course of his dealings. This includes VAT, PAYE, social security contributions and income tax deducted from interest and other payments.

5.100 If a trading loss is incurred by the receiver continuing to trade in order to sell a business as a going concern, it may be possible for such loss incurred in the last twelve months of trading to be set against any profits earned by the company during the three years preceding those twelve months.

5.101 The disposal of assets by the receiver may give rise to chargeable gains. Under the Capital Gains Tax Act 1979 (CGTA 79) Section 23(2), such gains are assessable on the company and not on the receiver.

Payment of Liquidation Expenses

5.102 If a receiver is appointed when the company is in liquidation he will, under the rule in *Re Barleycorn Enterprises Ltd* [1970] 2 All ER 155, be liable to pay liquidation expenses out of the proceeds of the floating charge (but after his own remuneration and expenses).

Chapter 6

Continuing to Trade and Hiving-Down

6.1   Reference has already been made (see paragraph 1.5 above) to the crucial importance of the decision by the receiver as to whether or not to continue trading. Whilst there may be many inducements to continue trading, the dangers of so doing should not be ignored. The receiver has a statutory duty to the preferential creditors (IA s 40) and, if by trading on and making losses, he worsens their position, he can be held personally liable to make good any resulting shortfall (*Westminster City Council v Haste* [1950] Ch 442). On the other hand, he has no duty to trade on simply to preserve the company's goodwill (*Re B Johnston and Co (Builders) Ltd* [1955] 2 All ER 775).

The Short Term

6.2   It will often be advantageous to continue to trade, perhaps for one or two weeks (unless it is immediately obvious that no advantage is to be gained by so doing). This is particularly relevant to manufacturing companies where completed work-in-progress is likely to realise a better value as finished goods than in its unfinished state at the date of the receiver's appointment. The initial one or two-week period will give the receiver time to gather the information he requires before making a decision on whether or not to continue trading for a longer period.

6.3   Certain factors must be carefully examined, however, before deciding to trade even in the short term. The receiver must satisfy himself that there will be a cash advantage in finishing the work in progress. He must determine the costs of completion, paying particular attention to his stock requirements and any encumbrances that there might be on such stock. He must also ensure that the workforce is willing and able to carry out the work and also that, at the end of the day, there is a customer who is willing and able to pay for the goods.

The Long Term

6.4   By far the greatest justification for continuing to trade for anything more than one or two weeks will be the prospect of a sale of all or part of the business as a going concern. Before a receiver can decide whether this is a worthwhile prospect, he must satisfy himself on various points.

6.5   First, there must be a genuine interest being shown in the business by parties who are able to raise the necessary finance.

6.6   Second, to justify the risk of continuing to trade, the realisable value of the business as a going concern must substantially exceed the break-up value of the assets.

6.7   Third, the business must have a future. Whilst the directors may well be confident of the prospects of the company despite the fact that it has been making substantial losses, the receiver will need to satisfy a potential purchaser that there is indeed a market for the product or service concerned, and that, despite its history, the business can be turned around and be profitable.

6.8   Finally, the receiver must be sure that he has the financial resources to continue the trade for the period necessary to achieve a sale of the business, and that he can do so without deterioration in the value of the assets available for the creditors at the time of his appointment. Financial resources will be more readily available if the appointor is a bank.

Gathering Information

6.9   During the initial period, the receiver and his staff must gather together a great deal of information about the company. Whilst certain areas will be more important in individual cases, in practice all the information tends to be gathered simultaneously.

6.10 Much information can be obtained from interviews with the directors and senior employees. It should be possible from such interviews to build up a broad picture of the business; in particular its products or services, its market and the competition. The senior personnel may also be able to identify prospective purchasers of the business and may even make an offer themselves (see paragraphs 7.18 to 7.22 below). The assistance of the directors may also be sought in the valuation of certain assets.

6.11 These interviews are also the receiver's opportunity to assess the strengths and weaknesses of the management team on whose ability he will have to rely to a large degree during a period of trading. The receiver will find it useful to understand the management structure so that established channels of communication and chains of command can be followed and be seen to be continuing to operate. This is important, since should the receiver decide to arrange for the company to continue trading, one of the major factors on which success will depend will be the co-operation and the motivation of the management and staff.

6.12 Professional valuers must be instructed to estimate both break-up and going-concern values in respect of the physical assets. Property belonging to third parties, or subject to reservation of title clauses and not paid for, should be identified and excluded. To these values must be added a valuation of book debts and investments. In addition, the value of a business as a going concern may be augmented by intangible assets such as patents, trade marks and know-how which are unlikely to have a break-up value. Once the above information is all to hand, schedules of the value of the business can be prepared both on break-up and going-concern bases, and by incorporating the debts due to the secured and preferential creditors, a comparison can be made of the likely recovery to result from either method of disposal (see appendix D).

6.13 The nature of the product or service should be carefully considered. This is to identify the risks involved in manufacture of the product, or supply of the service, and the prospect of liability being incurred in the event of failure of the product after sale, or as a consequence of the supply of the service. Construction contracts, for example, are invariably fraught with inherent dangers and should be given very careful consideration.

6.14 Contracts, licences, leases and rental agreements should be examined to ascertain which, if any, may have terminated as a result of the receiver's appointment. The importance to the business of those which may have terminated should be considered. Onerous contracts should be abandoned by the receiver, bearing in mind that a breach can only result in an unsecured claim against the company or set-off against monies due on other contracts from the same customer (see paragraph 5.13 et seq above).

6.15 Sales forecasts will be required. These will have to be examined very critically. Order books may include unconfirmed or long overdue orders which are unlikely to result in sales. Customers may have found alternative sources of supply in the light of the financial problems of the company or may have doubts as to continued supply or the servicing of long-term contracts.

6.16 The pricing policy should be reviewed. Products may have been sold in the past at a loss and the possibility of increasing selling prices should be examined. If the receiver decides to continue the trade, he will need to obtain from each customer an undertaking that payments will be made in full for goods delivered, without set-off of any pre-receivership debts which might be due to the customer (see paragraph 5.55 above).

6.17 Profitable and unprofitable areas should be identified. It may be that a profitable part of the business can be sold separately as a going concern, leaving the rest to be disposed of piecemeal.

6.18 Stocks should be physically checked to ensure that there are no major shortages which would result in an increase in production outlay if discovered later. The validity of reservation of title claims should also be considered to see whether the relevant goods are available for continued trading. Careful consideration must be given to the position of suppliers of vital materials. Monopoly suppliers will try to insist on payment in full of their pre-receivership bills before they will continue supply. This should be resisted on grounds of equity to others, but 'premium' prices may be negotiated.

6.19 Production resources must be examined. Machinery must have sufficient capability and be sufficiently reliable to meet the production programme. Professional advice might be valuable in this respect.

6.20 The opinions of the workforce should be sought, via their representatives, and trade union officials should be consulted as to the receiver's proposals particularly with regard to operational cut-backs. Discussions should be open and frank and, if the case is put clearly, co-operation should be forthcoming. In the current economic climate, the prospect of continuing to trade and the preservation of employment should encourage support for the receiver. It can happen that there is skill and willingness within the workforce previously unrecognised by the management which, if harnessed, can dramatically improve the performance of the business. The importance of good staff relations cannot be over-emphasised.

6.21 One final aspect to be explored is the possibility of Government assistance. The Department of Industry should be contacted to see what grants or subsidies might be applicable to the particular circumstances of the business, the nature of the product, or the geographical location of the business. Where there is a prospect of large redundancies, for example, the Department might exercise its discretion in granting specific aid. Assistance might also be available from the Department of Employment or the EEC. The extent of assistance available will vary with the circumstances of each case.

Communication with Banks

6.22 Once all the information has been gathered, profit forecasts and cash flow forecasts should be drawn up for the periods of trading under consideration. Initially, these might be for one- and three-month periods. Armed with these forecasts, a receiver will then be in a position to make his recommendations to the debenture holder, whose approval it is prudent to obtain if a decision to trade is indicated. Cash flow forecasts should highlight the peak cash needs so that the bank can be warned of any further commitment required.

6.23 If trading is continued, the receiver must then ensure that the debenture holder receives regular progress reports and that major divergences from the original forecasts are brought to the debenture holder's attention.

6.24 A close relationship between a receiver and the bank appointing him is imperative. Once the appointment is made, whilst the ultimate responsibility for action will rest with the receiver, it will be essential to establish good communications at all times to ensure that the bank is kept fully informed of everything that affects its position and, conversely, to ensure that the receiver is always aware of the bank's views.

6.25 A bank may have wider interests than the recovery of the immediate debt at risk. These include the welfare of other customers and the bank's standing in the community at large. Where circumstances and the interests of other parties allow, the receiver should always give his appointing bank the opportunity to consider a course of action which may result in a less certain recovery of its debt but may better satisfy these wider interests. The rights of other creditors and guarantors of the debenture must of course not be prejudiced in so doing and, furthermore, the receiver should obtain an indemnity from the bank if such a course is adopted.

Hiving-Down

6.26 As mentioned in paragraph 5.21 above, it may be desirable to limit the liability which might otherwise fall on a receiver by transferring the business to a newly formed subsidiary company. This process is known as 'hiving-down'. It does not remove the assets from the creditors' control, as the creditors still retain the benefit of those assets through the shares that the insolvent company owns in its new subsidiary. Hiving-down can be particularly desirable where a company trading in receivership is likely to be placed into liquidation, thus ending the receiver's agency and making him a principal on all transactions.

6.27 There can be other advantages to a receiver in hiving-down, some of which are noted in the following paragraphs, but hiving-down should not be regarded as an automatic procedure to be adopted in all trading cases. There are many complex legal and tax implications and no hiving-down should be undertaken without prior consultation with professional advisors.

6.28 Another purpose of hiving-down is to preserve the tax benefit of trading losses available to be carried forward under ICTA Section 177, so as to enhance the value of the business to the purchaser, although losses that can be carried forward are restricted to the extent that creditors are not paid in full (Finance Act 1986 s 42 and Sch 10). For this purpose, the hiving-down must involve the whole of the trade and undertaking and must take place before the presentation of a winding-up petition, or the passing of a winding-up resolution. Care, however, must be taken to ensure that the likely benefit from the inclusion of the tax losses in the sale exceeds any claim for repayment of corporation tax which could otherwise be obtained on a terminal loss claim arising on a cessation of the old trade. Any capital losses will remain in the transferor company.

6.29 As mentioned in paragraph 6.28 above, the hiving-down must take place before liquidation if tax losses are to be transferred. Even if the business is hived down before the appointment of a receiver the contracts of all the staff employed in the business will be transferred to the new company only when the hive-down company leaves the group (TU(PE)R).

The Method of Hiving-Down

6.30 Each hiving-down agreement should be drafted by the receiver's solicitors to meet the particular circumstances of each case. Different businesses can be transferred to separate hive-down companies.

6.31 A hive-down company is a useful vehicle for the disposal of the trading assets and goodwill on a going-concern basis, but legal advice should be taken to ensure that the hiving-down will not result in a breach of any leases, licences or other agreements on which the company depends for the continuance of its business, or in the breach of the terms of any charge granted to secured creditors.

6.32 The hive-down company should always be a new subsidiary formed or acquired specially for the purpose. The costs of acquiring such a company are relatively low and the use of a new company will avoid the time and costs involved in investigating the financial positions of existing dormant subsidiaries.

6.33 Any company acquired from company registration agents at short notice will have at best a completely neutral name. It can, however, adopt the original company's name (without the words 'Limited' or 'Public Limited Company' or their Welsh equivalents) as a trading style, provided that its true name is also shown on its stationery. (See also paragraph 7.21 below).

6.34 For convenience, the new company's accounting reference date should coincide with either the insolvent company's accounting reference date, or the date to which the receiver's accounts will have to be prepared.

6.35 Provided that the hive-down company is registered for VAT purposes with effect from the date of the transfer of the business or earlier, no VAT will be chargeable on the transfer of the trading assets. The hiving-down agreement (and any contract for the sale of the hive-down company to an eventual purchaser) should specifically state that the consideration for the assets is exclusive of VAT. If this is not done, the eventual purchaser could subsequently seek to claim that the consideration was inclusive of VAT and apply to HM Customs and Excise for recovery by way of VAT input, leaving the receiver with a potential liability to account for the apparent VAT element on the sale.

6.36 It is recommended that most of the consideration for the assets being transferred (except for a nominal amount to be attributed to share capital) be expressly stated to be left outstanding on a loan account between the two companies, and determinable by the receiver's firm acting as experts and not as arbitrators. This avoids possible stamp duty and capital gains problems. The valuation can be formally made at the time of ultimate sale to reflect the price negotiated with the eventual purchaser. The purchaser will then take over the shares in the hive-down company at par and advance to it the funds necessary to discharge the loan account.

6.37 Contracts of employment should not be transferred to the hive-down company. If they were, the employees' accrued rights would also be transferred to the new company and, since that company is solvent, would thus be payable in full. Under TU(PE)R, the employees' contracts will be automatically transferred to the hive-down company immediately before the completion of the sale to the ultimate purchaser. Employees that the purchaser intends to employ should be dismissed prior to the transfer of the business to the purchaser and then they can be re-engaged by the new company shortly afterwards (see paragraphs 4.33 to 4.36 above).

6.38 Similarly, freehold and leasehold property should not be transferred. To do so could give rise to a stamp duty liability, and make the hive-down company liable to pay tax on the capital gains on those assets once it is sold to an eventual purchaser. Book debts should not be transferred for to do so would also create a stamp duty liability.

Further Practical Aspects of Hiving-Down

6.39 The appointment of directors for the hive-down company is a matter to be determined by the receiver. Those appointed will normally be his own senior employees. He should be wary of appointing directors and senior employees of the insolvent company because of his statutory duty to report on the conduct of those directors.

6.40 The registered office of the hive-down company should be the same as that of the company in receivership. The secretary will normally be a member of the receiver's staff.

6.41 Separate accounting records must be maintained for the hive-down company. If the subsidiary is sold, it will be necessary to hand these records to the purchaser. A separate bank account will also be required.

6.42 The trade may be conducted by the new company as principal or as agent for its insolvent parent. If the second alternative is adopted, the advantage of avoiding certain liabilities (see paragraph 5.19 et seq above) may be lost.

6.43 Whichever alternative is adopted, an inter-company account must be maintained between the insolvent company and the hive-down company. This will be needed to reflect transactions entered into by either the insolvent or hive-down company on behalf of the other and particularly to recharge to the hive-down any costs relating to employees retained by the insolvent company for the benefit of the hive-down.

6.44 Arrangements should be made for the hive-down company to collect the book debts on the insolvent company's behalf. If this is done, all funds received from debtors should be put into a separate bank account and transferred to the receiver as soon as possible.

Eventual Sale of the Hived-Down Business

6.45 This can be effected by the purchaser acquiring the shares in the hive-down company and undertaking to procure the immediate repayment of the inter-company loan account. The hiving-down agreement can, if necessary, be amended immediately before the sale to reflect any alterations requested by the purchaser. The amendment may be effected by a written agreement (or by a deed, if the original hiving-down agreement was under seal) executed by the parties to the original agreement.

6.46 The purchaser of the business may not wish to take over the hive-down company (see paragraph 7.21 below). In this case, the assets may be sold on to him by the hive-down company or the hiving-down agreement may be revoked. To avoid tax and legal complications, it may also be advisable to revoke a hiving-down agreement if no purchaser can be found.

Chapter 7

Disposals and Reorganisations

7.1   In this chapter we outline methods available to the receiver for realising the assets under his control. In theory, there are three courses open to him. He can:

(a)   realise assets piecemeal, without attempting to secure the continuance of trade;
(b)   dispose of the viable parts of the business, or the business as a whole, as a going concern;
(c)   seek a buyer for the whole company, on a basis which ensures creditors are taken on and which leaves something for the shareholders.

7.2   As regards course (b) in paragraph 7.1 above, the arguments for continuing the business prior to disposal were examined in chapter 6 and it was emphasised there that this option was only attractive if there were the prospect of disposal as a going concern. Otherwise, piecemeal realisation is the proper course. As regards course (c), it rarely occurs in practice that the receiver is able to sell at such a price that shareholders receive anything, since others will probably have tried before him and failed, but there will be occasions when subsidiary companies can be disposed of where they are profitable entities (see paragraph 7.24 et seq below).

Methods of Sale

7.3   Unless the debenture deed provides otherwise, the administrative receiver has the power to sell or otherwise dispose of the property of the company (IA Sch 1). He may do this in any of the following ways:

(a)   *Sale by Private Treaty*

This method may be disadvantageous in that it can be several months before a binding contract of sale is signed. It will, however, often be the only way of dealing with the complications of going-concern sales.

(b)   *Sale by Tender*

As well as being inexpensive, a sale of major assets by tender often realises proceeds in excess of those obtainable at an auction sale, since a potential buyer normally has no indication of prices offered by a competitor. This method is valuable when there is strong competition to purchase an asset.

(c)   *Sale by Auction*

The advantage here is that the purchaser buys on the basis of a contract incorporated in the auction particulars. An auction is generally suitable for small assets or substantial assets for which there is a wide market.

In some circumstances the mortgagee may of course sell the assets himself.

7.4   A receiver usually protects himself by obtaining a professional valuation before disposing of material assets. Where a precise valuation is not possible for a sale by private treaty, it is advisable to ask the valuers to confirm, before entering into any commitment, that no higher price could reasonably be expected in the circumstances. It is also usually advisable to obtain from the valuers an inventory of the assets, stating the value allocated to each item.

7.5   In all circumstances it is important to remember that the mortgagee or receiver is under a duty to obtain the true market value of the mortgaged property when either of them exercises their power of sale (*American Express Banking Corporation v Hurley* [1985] 3 All ER 564). It is therefore appropriate to obtain specialist advice when dealing with the disposal of any specialised businesses or assets.

Hire Purchase Disposals

7.6   Before disposing of any equipment, the receiver must ensure that the equipment is not on hire purchase, and is, without doubt, the property of the company. If he sells equipment on hire purchase or otherwise not belonging to the company, he will be liable personally for damages for conversion. Such damages are normally based on the market value of the articles he has sold; but, in the case of hire purchase agreements, they will not normally exceed the amount of the outstanding balance due under the hire purchase agreement (see also paragraph 5.83 et seq above).

7.7   If there is any doubt concerning the validity of any hire purchase agreement, legal advice should be obtained (e.g. see paragraph 8.5 below).

7.8   Valuation of property subject to hire purchase may show a surplus of value of the property over the outstanding instalments. If the receiver is satisfied that he will more than recover the sum expended from the sale of the property concerned (in some cases the hire purchase company will quote a reduced sum for an immediate settlement) he may be justified in continuing to pay the outstanding instalments or discharging the hire purchase agreement. Such a course of action could only be adopted with the consent of the hire purchase company (see paragraph 5.83 et seq above) and is often frustrated by the owner's right to consolidate all contracts with him.

7.9   The debenture holder is sometimes able to claim that machinery, whether or not on hire purchase, has become part of the mortgaged real property by being fixed or attached to the land. The matter is, however, extremely complex and the receiver should always obtain legal advice. In the last resort, the question is a physical one and can probably only be resolved after examination, by an expert, of the equipment concerned.

Disposal of Charged Property

7.10   The receiver has the power to apply to the court for an order authorising him to dispose of any property subject to a charge that ranks ahead of that of his appointor (IA s 43(1)). He must satisfy the court that the disposal would be likely to promote a more beneficial realisation of assets than would otherwise be the case. When the venue for the hearing has been fixed the receiver must advise the chargeholder (IR 3.31(2)). It will be a condition of the order that the secured creditor shall receive the net proceeds of sale or the market value, if higher, the difference being made up from receivership funds (IA s 43(3)). This should enable receivers to include in the sale of a business factory premises which may be subject to a mortgage.

7.11   Forthwith after the making of the order, the receiver must give notice to the holder of the security and as soon as the receiver has been sent the two sealed copies by the court he must send one of those to the security holder (IR 3.31(3) and (4)). He must also send an office copy of the order to the Registrar of Companies, together with a form 3.8 (see appendix H.9) within 14 days of the making of the order (IA s 43(5)).

Sale as a Going Concern

7.12 The receiver may sell, as a going concern, the assets, goodwill, and undertaking in whole or in part, without transferring the liabilities, which then remain the company's responsibility. The course adopted will depend on the open market break-up value of the assets as compared with their going-concern value. The going-concern value will in turn depend on an assessment of the viability of the business and the costs that may be incurred in carrying it on until it can be sold (see chapter 6).

7.13 Prospective purchasers may approach the receiver or may be identified by the company's management. The receiver will often instruct his valuation agents to find a buyer for the business and advertising may be necessary. If this is the case, great care must be taken to avoid contravening the provisions of the Prevention of Fraud (Investments) Act 1958, under which, in certain circumstances, it can be an offence to invite persons to enter into an agreement to acquire securities. It should therefore be made clear in any advertisement that it is a business which is for sale and not shares in a company. This does not of course prohibit the receiver from eventually selling shares at the purchaser's request (see also paragraph 6.36 et seq above).

7.14 Where several interested parties are forthcoming, the receiver will find it advisable to prepare a package of information about the company. In the preparation and distribution of such sale packages, due consideration should again be given to the Prevention of Fraud (Investments) Act 1958 and care must be taken not to give away trade secrets to competitors. Since the receiver is unlikely to be familiar with every aspect of the business, he should consider the advisability of disclaiming liability for any inaccuracies in the information contained in the package.

7.15 The sales package should include:

(a)   a brief history of the company including recent and projected trading results, and cash flow projections where these are relevant;
(b)   a description of the products backed by sales brochures where applicable;
(c)   a list of the plant and machinery (usually a copy of the valuers' inventory with the values blocked out);
(d)   details of the stock and work-in-progress;
(e)   a description of the company's premises;
(f)   details of major contracts, licences, patents and trade marks; and
(g)   numbers of staff employed and brief details of each of the senior managers and directors.

The package should be accompanied by a letter inviting offers.

7.16 Parties expressing serious interest may wish to visit the company's premises and may require further information. At this point, the receiver should meet the prospective purchasers and negotiations can commence and be continued until agreement in principle is reached.

7.17 It is advisable for a number of reasons, especially taxation, that upon the sale of a business or of a group of assets, each particular asset be allocated a proportion of the sale price, in agreement with the purchaser. It is preferable that the allocation be negotiated at the time that the disposal is made, or for the agreement to provide a means of arriving at it. Stamp duty implications need to be considered in allocating the consideration. The interests of the vendor and the purchaser may conflict and consultation with the receiver's tax advisers is vital at all stages.

Management Buy-Outs

7.18 A receiver may well receive an offer for a going concern from the existing management, and indeed may be persuaded to trade on in anticipation of such an offer. Whilst management buy-outs are not a new phenomenon in the UK, it is only in recent years that they have become a common occurrence; indeed to such an extent that a Management Buy-Out Association has been formed to advise managers contemplating a buy-out.

7.19 A management buy-out is quite simply the purchase of a business from its existing owners by its executive managers with the backing of financial institutions. The institutions usually provide the bulk of the purchase consideration in the form of loans and preference capital, leaving the managers to take a controlling stake in the equity for a relatively small contribution to the total purchase consideration. CA 85 Section 155 has removed a major stumbling block in the structuring of such transactions by suitably relaxing the provisions previously contained in CA 48 Section 54 which prohibited the provision of security by a company to finance the purchase of its own shares.

7.20 Sometimes an offer by the management is the only one available to a receiver. The major advantage to a receiver from selling a business to its management is that such a transaction offers the prospect of preserving the future of the business and therefore the employment of its workforce. In addition, it minimises handover problems following a sale. There can however be disadvantages also. For example, the directors have a clear conflict of interest if, as potential purchasers of the business, they also have a hand in assisting the receiver in running the business and/or in dealing with other prospective purchasers.

7.21 It must be borne in mind that the administrative receiver has to consider the conduct of the directors (see paragraphs 9.37 et seq). It is also important that he obtains a proper price for the business when dealing with them or their representatives. The management must also be advised of the restrictions on the re-use of company names (IA s 216). A person who was within the preceding twelve months a director or shadow director of a company that has gone into insolvent liquidation, cannot, without the approval of the court, within a period of five years beginning with the date of the liquidation, become a director or take part in, either directly or indirectly, the affairs of a company known by the same or similar name. Whilst 'receivership' is not 'insolvent liquidation' directors should appreciate that a company in administrative receivership might at some point be put in liquidation.

7.22 To avoid contravening Section 320 of the Companies Act 1985, directors should consider resigning their directorships before commencing negotiations with the receiver. However the resignation is not necessary if the transaction is approved by the shareholders.

Sale of Tax Losses

7.23 If the company has unutilised tax losses, there is the possibility of these being allowed against future profits of the same trade carried on by a new subsidiary, following a hive-down (see chapter 6). There can be circumstances where the value of tax losses is substantial, but expert tax advice is needed in most cases.

Subsidiary Companies

7.24 Subsidiary companies are often a party to the debenture, charging their own assets to secure the advance from the lender. A receiver appointed under such a debenture will probably be appointed also to be receiver of the subsidiaries. Acting in this capacity he may be empowered to sell the assets of each company. He must, however, maintain separate accounts for the realisation of the assets of each company, and ensure that before the monies of a company are used to repay the debenture holder under the floating charge, the preferential creditors of that company are paid first from the realisation of that company's assets.

7.25 Generally, each company is jointly and severally liable under the debenture for the principal monies and interest. The actions of the receiver might well, therefore, give rise to complex claims between the companies themselves, as it is most unlikely that they will contribute equally to the repayment of the debenture holder. However, those claims do not affect the receiver; he may realise those assets which are most easily realisable and, after payment of preferential creditors in the case of a floating charge, account to his debenture holder. Unrealised assets or surplus realisations should be returned to the individual companies or their liquidators, as appropriate, unless the terms of the debenture stock charge provide that the surplus should be returned to the parent company (see *Brown v Cork and another* Court of Appeal [1985] BCLC 363). This type of charge is normally encountered in the case of a debenture stock issued to the public and listed on the Stock Exchange, where the interests of the individual debenture stock holder are in the hands of a trustee, who will usually be one of the major insurance companies.

7.26 If the company has subsidiaries or associated investments and the appointment of a receiver does not extend to them, the receiver must ensure that, where the subsidiary continues to trade, he is provided with all appropriate management information. If the subsidiary has a value he may wish to dispose of the shares, but he must always take care not to arrange for his nominee to become a director or influence the existing directors such that he be deemed a shadow director of the subsidiary with all the onerous consequences.

Chapter 8

The Receiver-Creditor Relationship

8.1   This chapter examines the relationship of the receiver with all types of creditors and, in the process, classifies them according to their statutory ranking and any other special considerations.

8.2   Creditors can be broadly divided into six classes:

(a)   Secured.
(b)   Special.
(c)   Preferential.
(d)   Guaranteed.
(e)   Unsecured.
(f)   Judgment.

Secured Creditors

8.3   These are creditors who have advanced monies secured over the assets of the company.

8.4   The debenture holders who have appointed the receiver will fall into this category. However, the receiver must ensure that there are no other secured creditors with a prior charge. If there are prior charges, the rights of their holders must be recognised by the receiver even though he was not appointed by the secured creditor concerned. There may also be a secured creditor with a second fixed charge ranking after the fixed charge of the debenture holder client but ahead of his floating charge. Again, such rights must be recognised.

Special Creditors

Hire Purchase Companies

8.5   Hire purchase companies are not, technically, secured creditors since the goods hired do not belong to the company in the first instance. The hire purchase company's right to repossession, however, means that its claims are in an analogous position. When an asset has been first sold by the company prior to receivership, and then made the subject of a hire purchase or other arrangement between the company and the hire purchase company concerned, without the transaction as a whole being registered as a bill of sale, the receiver may sometimes be able to attack the validity of this transaction. Legal advice should be sought in such circumstances. (See paragraph 5.83 et seq above.)

Landlords

8.6   If there are neither arrears of rent nor breaches of covenant, the landlord is not entitled to terminate a lease upon the appointment of a receiver, unless the lease specifically provides that he may do so. Even if the lease does provide for forfeiture on the appointment of a receiver, it may be possible for the receiver to utilise Section 146 of the Law of Property Act 1925 or simply apply for release from forfeiture on equitable grounds. Legal advice should be sought. Although the receiver is not a party to the lease and not personally liable thereunder, he may have to pay the rent arrears and perform the necessary obligations if he wishes to avoid forfeiture of the lease. He is not obliged to pay any rent if he considers it advantageous to allow the landlord to forfeit the property (*Hand v Blow* [1901] 2 Ch 721). If there are arrears of rent, one remedy that the landlord has is a right to levy 'distress'.

Distress for Rent

Introduction

8.7   Distress for rent may be summarised as the right of a landlord to seize goods found on premises let by him to a tenant whose rent for those premises is in arrears. A landlord may levy distress at any time when rent on the premises is overdue. A landlord may thus levy distress for rent payable in advance at any time following the day on which it should have been paid (*Dibble v Bowater* [1853] 2 E & B 564). The landlord is not required to serve a demand for payment before he levies distress. It is, however, arguable that distress cannot be levied where the amount of the rent has not been ascertained (*United Scientific Holdings Ltd v Burnley Borough Council* [1978] AC 904), which could restrict a landlord's rights where a rent review is outstanding. It is important to note that distress is an *alternative* to legal action through the courts. Once a landlord has obtained judgment for the rent he loses his right to distrain (*Chancellor v Webster* [1893] 9 TLR 568).

The landlord must levy distress in person or through a person authorised to act as a bailiff by a certificate in writing under the hand of a County Court judge (Section 7, Law of Distress Amendment Act 1888). Since a company can only act through agents it must employ a certificated bailiff for this purpose. A person can be certificated for the purposes of levying one particular distress (Rule 3(1), Distress for Rent Rules 1983) but in practice this is rare.

A bailiff's authority to levy distress normally takes the form of a so-called 'distress warrant' signed by or on behalf of the landlord, but written authority is not strictly necessary.

The person levying distress may not use force to enter the premises (*American Concentrated Must Corporation v Hendry* [1983] 62 LJQB 388). Once he has gained access, however, he may use force to break open doors where necessary (*Lee v Gansel* [1774] 1 Cowp 1) and may use force to re-enter the premises once he has left them (*Bannister v Hyde* [1860] 2 E & E 627).

Goods Liable to Seizure

8.8   Originally the landlord could levy distress on any goods found on the premises which were capable of being removed and restored in their identical condition. Distress therefore cannot be levied on:

(a)   fixtures, since they are legally part of the freehold (*Pitt v Shew* [1821] 4 B & Ald 206);
(b)   perishable goods (*Simpson v Hartopp* [1744] Willes 512); or
(c)   coins and notes, unless it could be proved that any restored to the tenant were the same ones that had been removed.

In the case of an agricultural tenancy, however, distress can be levied on the crops and cattle whether already harvested or not (Sections 8 and 9, Distress for Rent Act 1737).

The following are also exempt from distress:

(a)   non-physical assets; thus the seizure of letters patent does not confer any right to use the patent or stop the patentee exploiting his invention (*British Mutoscope and Biograph Co Ltd v Homer* [1901] 1 Ch 671);
(b)   business books and records (*Gauntlett v King* [1857] 3 CB(NS) 59);

(c)   items actually in use (*Field v Adames* [1840] 12 Ad & El 649); and
(d)   goods already subject to execution (*Wharon v Naylor* [1848] 12 QB 673).

The exclusion of items in use is intended to avoid a breach of the peace. It is therefore possible that a landlord or bailiff could levy distress on such items if he could peaceably persuade the person concerned to stop using them.

Seizure

8.9   Distress is completed by seizing the goods, but this can be accomplished by seizing hold of one article and stating it to be taken in distress in the name of all (*Dod v Monger* [1704] 6 Mod Rep 215). Alternatively, seizure may be accomplished by preventing removal of the goods (*Cramer & Co Ltd v Mott* [1870] LR 5 QB 357).

Once distress has been levied the goods are said to be impounded. The person distraining may remove them to a place of safety or leave them on the premises. If they are left on the premises then either a man may be left in physical possession of them or the tenant may be asked to sign a 'walking possession agreement' in the form specified in the Distress for Rent Rules 1983. The fee for leaving a man in possession is only £2.50 per day, so it is likely that the goods will be removed at the earliest opportunity unless a walking possession agreement is signed.

The goods seized cannot be sold until the landlord or bailiff has served on the tenant a notice in the prescribed form listing the goods seized, setting out the amount for which distress has been levied and the fees and charges payable and stating when they will be sold (Section 1, Distress for Rent Act 1689 and Distress for Rent Rules 1983).

A tenant faced with an actual or threatened distress which is illegal may apply for an injunction (*Walsh v Lonsdale* [1882] 21 Ch D 9). If he wishes to challenge the distress and recover the goods in other circumstances he may do so by taking an action of 'replevin' in the county court on lodging security for the rent and costs in an amount fixed by the Registrar.

Evasion or Interference by the Tenant

8.10   In addition to the goods he finds on the premises, the landlord or bailiff may also levy distress on any goods belonging to the tenant that were fraudulently or clandestinely removed from the premises at any time within the preceding thirty days (Section 1, Distress for Rent Act 1737). The tenant and any person knowingly assisting him in the fraudulent or clandestine removal is also liable to pay the landlord twice the value of the goods removed (Section 3, Distress for Rent Act 1737).

Removal of seized goods by the tenant or by any other person who is aware of the distress constitutes 'poundbreach', entitling the landlord to exercise the right of 'recaption', i.e. the right to physically recover the goods. He is also entitled to damages. Poundbreach is a criminal offence (*Regina v Butterfield* [1893] 17 Cox CC 598).

It is considered that a tenant may continue to use impounded goods that have been left on the premises provided they are not consumed in the use. In theory seized goods cannot be sold, even in the ordinary course of trade. In practice the bailiff may be prepared to allow seized goods to be sold in the ordinary course of trade provided they are replaced with other goods of the same type at least equal in value.

Third Party Goods

8.11   The Law of Distress Amendment Act 1908 restricted a landlord's right to levy distress on third party property. Under Sections 4 and 4A of that Act, however, distress may still be levied on:

(a)   goods in the tenant's possession with the consent of the true owner in circumstances making the tenant their reputed owner;

(b)   goods subject to a bill of sale, hire purchase agreement or conditional sale agreement or subject to a consumer hire purchase agreement within the meaning of the Consumer Credit Act 1974;

(c)   goods belonging to any partner of the tenant;

(d)   goods belonging to a subtenant and for use in a business in which both the tenant and the subtenant have an interest;

(e)   goods belonging to a company and held in its offices on premises of which the tenant is its director, officer or employee; and

(f)   goods left in office or warehouse premises which have not been removed by their true owner within one month of service on him of a notice requiring him to do so.

Distress may also be levied on goods belonging to a subtenant whose subtenancy was created in breach of the terms on which the tenant held the premises (Section 5, Law of Distress Amendment Act 1908).

The landlord or his bailiff is under no duty to refrain from levying distress on exempt third party goods. The onus is on the third party to claim the benefit of the exemption (Section 1, Law of Distress Amendment Act 1908). To do so he must serve on the landlord or the bailiff a written declaration:

(a)   that the goods are his property or in his lawful possession;

(b)   that the tenant has no right of property or beneficial interest in them; and

(c)   that they do not fall within any of the exceptions specified in the Act.

An inventory of the goods claimed by the third party must be attached. Making a false declaration is a criminal offence (Section 5, Perjury Act 1911).

Where the goods belong to a subtenant he must at the same time deliver to the landlord a statement of the rent due from him to the tenant, setting out any arrears and the due dates and amounts of any future payments. He must also undertake to pay the landlord all sums due under his subtenancy until such time as the rent for which the distress was levied or was to be levied has been discharged in full (Section 1, Law of Distress Amendment Act 1908).

The fact that goods may be subject to fixed or floating charges does not exclude them from distress. A landlord may levy distress even after an administrative receiver has been appointed (*Purcell v Queensland Public Curator* [1922] 31 CLR 220, an Australian case).

Hive-Down Companies (see chapter 6)

8.12   It is doubtful whether the transfer of the business and assets to a hive-down company would protect the assets from distress by a landlord, particularly as the hive-down company will normally be a subtenant of the premises in breach of a covenant in the original lease and it will be at least arguable that both the hive-down company and the insolvent company have an interest in the business.

It is possible that the transfer of assets to a hive-down company without either the transfer of the business or the creation of a subtenancy would defeat any future distress by the landlord, but this course of action is not recommended.

Liens

Repairer's Lien

8.13   The term 'repairer's lien' is self-explanatory; it is a particular lien enforceable in a receivership. Where such a lien is claimed, the receiver should take the following steps:

(a)   He should verify that the lien is valid, i.e. he should ensure that:

> (i) it is based upon the actual possession of the asset by the person claiming the lien or based upon the transfer of possession from that person with his right of lien expressly reserved;
>
> (ii) it involves the exercise of skill and labour by the repairer who is claiming the lien; and
>
> (iii) it involves the skill and labour charged for becoming embodied in the particular chattel over which the lien is claimed, and that such skill and labour has been authorised by the owner at or before the time the goods were transferred.

(b) He should decide whether the greater cash benefit to the receivership will result from:

> (i) payment in full of the amount claimed and recovery of the asset for disposal, or
>
> (ii) abandoning the asset to the holder of the lien.

(c) He should arrange to inform the holder of the lien of the decision taken, and to pay the amount claimed in appropriate cases.

Carrier's Lien

8.14 The company may have made a contract with a transport contractor or other temporary custodian of the company's goods ('bailee') the terms of which give the bailee a right of lien over the goods (see also appendix J.19). The contractual lien may be particular or general. A general lien may be exercised for all amounts owing by the owner to the bailee, whether or not they relate to the goods in question. Particularly in transport industries, standard conditions of contract often incorporate clauses conferring upon the transport contractor as bailee a right to a general lien.

Other Liens

8.15 Where a lien other than the repairer's lien is claimed, the contract under which the goods in question were transferred to the temporary custody of the bailee (the 'bail contract') must be examined. Standard conditions which may be found to form part of the contract often confer a right of both particular and general lien. Where there is a valid lien, the receiver must decide whether the value to the company of the goods within the lien justifies payment in full of the amount secured by the lien.

8.16 A person who has sold land (and possibly also shares or other types of property) to the company and has not been paid in full may have a vendor's lien over the property in question. The Sale of Goods Act 1979 gives an unpaid seller a lien on the grounds that the company should not be able to retain both the property and the money that ought to be paid for it. If such a lien is asserted, legal advice should be obtained.

8.17 In addition, solicitors are able to claim liens over title deeds and documents in their possession. These liens cannot be upset by the administrative receiver. However any person who holds property, books, papers or records belonging to the company, but cannot claim a lien, can be forced, on application to the court by the receiver, to release those items to him (IA s 234).

Trust Monies

8.18 It is frequently contended that monies paid to the company prior to the receiver's appointment are impressed with a trust. Many such claims are unwarranted. If no formal arrangements to establish a trust have been entered into or if the monies are no longer identifiable because the company's bank account was overdrawn at the date of the receiver's appointment, a claim of this nature is difficult to establish. Legal advice should be sought before conceding that a trust exists.

Nominated Sub-contractors

8.19 The receiver of a building contractor company may find that nominated sub-contractors will recover arrears due to them at the date of his appointment, by virtue of payments made by the client directly to the nominated sub-contractor out of monies due to the contractor. The rights of clients to make these payments will be governed by the terms of the particular contract. These terms must be carefully considered. (See paragraph 5.13 above.)

Preferential Creditors

8.20 Preferential creditors have priority over debenture holders with regard to assets covered by a floating charge (see paragraph 3.3 above) but not assets covered by a fixed charge. Preferential creditors are summarised in appendix E (IA s 386 and Sch 6) and the most significant categories are:

(a)   PAYE deductions.
(b)   Social security and pension contributions.
(c)   VAT.
(d)   Car tax.
(e)   Betting duties.
(f)   Employees' arrears of pay and holiday pay.

8.21 A receiver may advertise for preferential creditors if he considers this course to be prudent, but this in no way absolves him from responsibility for ensuring by other means that he has established all preferential claims.

8.22 Preferential claims in respect of banks require particular attention:

(a)   IA Schedule 6(11) clearly states that anyone who advances monies for the purpose of paying wages and salaries or accrued holiday remuneration of any employee is a preferential creditor to the extent that the preferential claims of the employees are diminished by payments out of such advances.

(b)   Where a company is in financial difficulties prior to the appointment of the receiver, a bank will often insist on opening a separate bank account to which all advances for the payment of wages and salaries will be debited. This is to avoid the possible loss of preference arising from the operation of the rule in *Clayton's Case* (1816) 1 Mer 572. The rule, as quoted in that case by the Master of the Rolls, is as follows:

> [In the case of a current account, there is] 'no room for any other appropriation than that which arises from the order in which the receipts and payments take place and are carried into the account. Presumably, it is the sum first paid in that is first drawn out. It is the first item on the debit side of the account that is discharged or reduced by the first item on the credit side. The appropriation is made by the very act of setting the two items against each other'.

> If a separate account is not opened, advances for the payment of wages by a bank may still be preferential. The bank is at liberty to examine the passbooks for the past four months prior to the appointment of the receiver, extracting all cheques known to it to be for wages or for salaries and the bank can claim preference for those payments, provided they are not deemed to have been repaid by the operation of the rule in *Clayton's Case*. The receiver must, however, deduct from the total of such cheques that part which was used for the payment of expenses, petty cash, and the like. He must also ensure that the maximum of £800 for wages or salaries for any one employee is not exceeded. This can happen, for example, where an employee is himself presenting a claim for arrears of commission over the relevant four months.

In summary, any wages/salaries payments up to the equivalent of £800 gross per employee, made within four months prior to the date of the receiver's appointment (subject to the employee's own claim), which form part of the overdraft in existence at the date of appointment, rank as preferential (see appendix E) to the extent that they have actually been paid from bank advances. It is important also to note that, when calculating the bank's claim, the *gross* amount must be deducted from the potential preferential claim and the *net* amount added to the bank's preferential claim. The reason for this is that the employee's own preferential claim has been reduced by the *gross* amount but the bank cannot claim more than the sum it actually paid which was the *net* figure.

Guaranteed Creditors

8.23 Under the insolvency provisions of EPCA, certain claims of the employees, which may or may not be preferential, will be paid out of the Redundancy Fund. The receiver, as agent for the Secretary of State for Employment, is required to agree the amount of the relevant claims with the employees and to forward details of the agreed claims to the local regional office of the Department of Employment, which administers the scheme. Payments in respect of the agreed claims are made out of the Redundancy Fund to the receiver, who is responsible for making any statutory deductions from the gross claims and for making the payment to the employees and to the appropriate authorities. A payment is made to the receiver in respect of the provision of these services (see paragraph 4.29 above and appendix F).

Unsecured Creditors

8.24 The prime duty of the receiver is to realise sufficient assets to make a full settlement to the debenture holders and preferential creditors. If settlement is made in full, the next group who can be beneficially or adversely affected by the receiver's actions are the unsecured creditors. The receiver should, however, consider the judgment in *G L Saunders* (see paragraph 10.14 below). Although the receiver is not directly responsible to the unsecured creditors, he may have a duty of care to them in certain circumstances (*Standard Chartered Bank v Walker* [1982] 1 WLR 1410) and (*American Express Banking Corporation v Hurley* [1985] 3 All ER 514).

8.25 The receiver has an obligation to notify creditors of his appointment and call a meeting within three months unless a liquidator has been appointed (IA ss 46 and 48). These matters are discussed more fully in chapter 9 (see paragraph 9.4 et seq below).

Judgment Creditors

8.26 Where execution has been levied by a creditor before the receiver's appointment, the receiver should immediately give notice to the bailiff who levied the execution. The receiver should claim the relevant assets, as the title of the debenture holder prevails over those execution creditors who have not completed their execution at the time of the receiver's appointment. It may, however, be necessary to pay the bailiff's costs. In case of doubt, legal advice should be sought (see appendix J.17).

8.27 A garnishee order is similarly defeated by the appointment of the receiver, except to the extent of monies already paid to the creditor (*Cairney v Back* [1906] 2 KB 746).

Chapter 9

The Statutory Duties of the Administrative Receiver

9.1   This chapter considers the statutory duties of the administrative receiver following acceptance of the appointment. The matters discussed are as follows:

(a)   Notice of appointment.
(b)   Notice to creditors.
(c)   Statement of affairs.
(d)   Statutory report.
(e)   Meeting of unsecured creditors.
(f)   Creditors committee.
(g)   Reports on directors.
(h)   VAT bad debt relief certificates.

Notice of Appointment

9.2   The administrative receiver must forthwith send a notice to the company stating the following matters (IA s 46(1)(a)) and (IR 3.2(2)):

(a)   the registered name of the company and registered number at the date of the appointment;
(b)   any other name by which the company has been registered in the twelve months preceding that date;
(c)   any name under which the company has traded at any time during those twelve months, if substantially different from its then registered name;
(d)   the name and address of the administrative receiver and the date of his appointment;
(e)   the name of the appointor;
(f)   the date and brief description of the charge under which the appointment was made;
(g)   a brief description of the assets, if any, excluded from the charge.

(See appendix I.2).

9.3   The administrative receiver must also advertise his appointment once in the Gazette and once in a newspaper circulating in the locality of the company's principal place of business (IR 3.2(3)). The matters to be stated in the advertisement are those specified in subparagraphs (a) to (e) above (IR 3.2(4)).

Notice to Creditors

9.4   Within twenty-eight days of his appointment (unless otherwise directed by the court) the administrative receiver must send a copy of the notice that has been sent to the company to all creditors of the company, so far as he is aware of their addresses (see appendix I.3). (IA s 46(1)(b)).

Statement of Affairs

9.5 Immediately on his appointment the administrative receiver is obliged to request some or all of the following to submit to him within 21 days a statement of affairs verified by affidavit (IA s 47(1) and (3)):

(a) those who are or have been officers of the company;
(b) those who have taken part in the company's formation at any time within one year of his appointment;
(c) those who are or have been in the company's employment during that year and in the administrative receiver's opinion capable of giving the required information;
(d) those who are or have been in the employment of a company which has been an officer of the company for any part of that year.

9.6 Those on whom such a request is served are described in the Rules as 'the deponents' (IR 3.3(2)). The request should be on Form 3.1 (see appendix H.2) which will give details (IR 3.3(3)):

(a) of the names and addresses of all others, if any, to whom a notice has been sent;
(b) of the time within which the statement must be delivered (which, unless extended by the administrative receiver, shall be 21 days);
(c) of the penalties for non-compliance with the request (IA s 47(6));
(d) of each deponent's duty to co-operate with the administrative receiver.

If requested by the deponents the administrative receiver must supply instructions for the preparation of the statement and the relevant forms (IR 3.3(4)).

Release from Duty to Submit Statement of Affairs and Extension of Time

9.7 The administrative receiver may at any time release a deponent from his obligation to provide a statement of affairs either at his own discretion or at the request of a deponent (IA s 47(5)). He may also extend the period for submission either when giving the notice or subsequently.

If the administrative receiver does not extend the period then the court, if it thinks fit, may do so (IA s 47(6)).

If a deponent requests a release or an extension of time and it is refused by the administrative receiver then he may apply to the court for it (IR 3.6(2)). The court may, if it thinks that no sufficient cause is shown for the application, dismiss it; but it shall not do so unless the applicant has had an opportunity to attend the court for an ex-parte hearing of which he has received seven days notice (IR 3.6(3)). If the application has not been dismissed following this then the court shall fix a venue for it to be heard and give notice to the deponent accordingly.

The deponent must, at least 14 days before the hearing, send to the administrative receiver a notice stating the venue and a copy of the application together with any evidence which he (the deponent) intends to present in support of it (IR 3.6(4)).

The administrative receiver may appear and be heard on the application; and whether or not he appears, he may file a written report of any matters which he considers ought to be drawn to the court's attention (IR 3.6(5)). If such a report is filed a copy of this must be sent to the deponent not later than 5 days before the hearing.

Sealed copies of any order made on the application are sent by the court to the deponent and the administrative receiver (IR 3.6(6)).

The applicant's costs must be paid by him unless the court otherwise orders (IR 3.6(7)).

9.8   The statement of affairs has to be submitted in Form 3.2 (see appendix H.3) and must contain all the particulars required by that form and must be verified by affidavit by the deponents.

The statement of affairs will contain (IA s 47(2)):

(a)   particulars of the company's assets, debts and liabilities;
(b)   the names and addresses of its creditors;
(c)   the securities held by them respectively;
(d)   the dates when the securities were respectively given;
(e)   any other information required.

9.9   The administrative receiver may require any of the persons mentioned in paragraph 9.5 to submit an affidavit of concurrence, stating that he concurs in the statement of affairs (IR 3.4(2)).

An affidavit of concurrence may be qualified in that the maker of the affidavit may not be in agreement with the deponent, or considers the statement to be erroneous or misleading, or he does not have the knowledge necessary for concurring with it (IR 3.4(3)).

The statement of affairs must be delivered to the administrative receiver by the deponent making the affidavit together with a copy of the verified statement, and any affidavit of concurrence together with a copy must similarly be delivered to the receiver (IR 3.4(4)).

9.10 Where the administrative receiver thinks that the conduct of the receivership would be prejudiced by a full disclosure of the statement of affairs to the registrar or other persons he may apply to the court for an order of limited disclosure (IR 3.5(1)). The court may then order that the statement or a specified part of it is not open to inspection other than with the leave of the court (IR 3.5(2)).

9.11 The costs of making the statement of affairs and affidavit are payable by the administrative receiver out of his receipts, in so far as he considers them reasonable (IR 3.7(1)).

Any decision by the administrative receiver is however subject to appeal to the court (IR 3.7(2)).

Statutory Report

9.12 Section 48 of the Act obliges the administrative receiver to prepare a report and both send it to creditors and lay it before a meeting of the unsecured creditors within three months of his appointment or such further time as the court may allow (IA s 48(1)). A copy of the report must also be sent to the Registrar of Companies within that period with Form 3.10 (see appendix H.11).

The report must cover the following matters (IA s 48(1)):

(a)   the events leading up to the administrative receiver's appointment, so far as he is aware of them;
(b)   the disposal or proposed disposal by him of any property of the company and the carrying on or proposed carrying on by him of any business of the company;
(c)   the amounts of principal and interest payable to the debenture holders by whom or on whose behalf he was appointed and the amounts payable to preferential creditors; and
(d)   the amount (if any) likely to be available for the payment of other creditors.

The report must also have attached a copy of the statement of affairs and copies of any affidavits of concurrence (IR 3.8(3)).

Whilst this may include the information required under (c) and (d) above, it should be remembered that the directors are responsible for the statement of affairs but the administrative receiver is responsible for the contents of his report. He will therefore have to confirm that the figures contained in the summary are a reasonable estimate or give his own estimates in the body of his report.

9.13 Should the statement of affairs not have been submitted by the time the report is finalised:

(a)   if the administrative receiver has extended the time for the submission of the statement, and the extended time has not expired, that fact should be mentioned in the report, together with a brief explanation as to why the extension was granted;

(b)   similarly, if the administrative receiver has released all the relevant people from their obligations to submit a statement of affairs, an explanation should be given;

(c)   if the extension of time was granted by the court, it is only necessary to mention that fact in the report, although in some cases it may also be appropriate to give the court's reasons for making the order;

(d)   if those concerned have simply failed to comply with their obligations to submit a statement of affairs within the time allowed, the administrative receiver should state that fact in the report and should also consider giving details of any actions taken by him as a result.

The administrative receiver need not include in his report 'any information the disclosure of which would seriously prejudice the carrying out by the administrative receiver of his functions' (see paragraph 9.10 above).

Copies of the report must be sent to the secured creditors (including secured creditors other than the appointor) and any trustee for secured creditors. Instead of sending copies to all the other creditors, the administrative receiver may advertise an address to which they may write for copies free of charge (IR 3.8(1)). The advertisement must be placed in the same newspaper as the original notice of his appointment.

If the statement of affairs or affidavits of concurrence, if any, were not submitted to the Registrar with the report, then as soon as available they should be sent with Form 3.3 (see appendix H.4). (IR 3.8(4)).

Meeting of Unsecured Creditors

9.14 The administrative receiver may apply to the court under Section 48(2) for an order dispensing with the meeting of creditors. He may only do so, however, if his report states that he intends to do so and is sent to creditors at least fourteen days before the hearing of his application (or the advertisement of the address to which creditors may apply for copies appears at least fourteen days before the hearing). The time and place of the hearing must be stated in the report or advertisement (IR 3.8(2)).

The administrative receiver must have regard to the convenience of the persons who are to attend when fixing the time and place of the meeting (IR 3.9(1)). It must be timed to commence between 1000 and 1600 on a business day, unless the court directs otherwise (IR 3.9(2)). All known creditors must be given at least fourteen days notice of the meeting (IR 3.9(3)) and notice must also be given in the newspaper used to advertise the administrative receiver's appointment (IR 3.9(6)).

The notice must:

(a)   include a statement that creditors who are fully secured are not entitled to attend or vote at the meeting (IR 3.9(5)); and

(b)   'state the effect of Rule 3.11(1)'. (IR 3.9(7)).

A draft form of notice, incorporating a statement regarding the effect of Rule 3.11(1) is shown in appendix I.5. The forms of proxy to be sent with the notice are as Form 8.3 (see appendix H.12). (IR 3.9(4)).

In order to reduce the number of questions that are likely to be raised, it is suggested that the administrative receiver prepares a report to be given orally at the meeting. There is no need to have such a report formally approved by the directors, although they should be given the opportunity to comment on it before the meeting.

Attendance at Meeting

9.15 Section 235(2) obliges various people connected with the company (basically the same people as can be called upon to submit a statement of affairs) to attend on the administrative receiver at such times as he may reasonably require. It is considered appropriate to require all persons who were directors of the company at any time within the six months preceding the date of appointment to attend the creditors meeting.

Conduct of Meeting

9.16 To comply with Rule 3.10 the meeting must be chaired by:

(a)   the administrative receiver;
(b)   another insolvency practitioner nominated by him in writing; or
(c)   'an employee of the administrative receiver or of his firm, who is experienced in insolvency matters'.

The directors present should be asked to join the chairman at the top table. The chairman should commence the proceedings by:

(i)   stating that the meeting has been convened in accordance with Section 48 of the Insolvency Act 1986;
(ii)   introducing himself and the others at the top table;
(iii) if he is not himself the administrative receiver, explaining why the meeting is not being chaired by the office holder;
(iv)   giving the names of any directors who were required to attend the meeting but have failed to do so, with any explanations they may have given; and
(v)   presenting the oral report.

After the conclusion of the report the creditors should be given the opportunity of asking questions. When the creditors do not have any further questions to raise, the chairman should enquire whether or not it is their wish to establish a committee.

Any committee must consist of not less than three and not more than five creditors (IR 3.16(1)). A body corporate can be a member of the committee but can only act through a duly authorised representative (IR 3.16(3)). If more than five creditors are nominated to serve it will be necessary to take a vote. A resolution appointing someone to the committee will be passed if a majority in value of those voting vote in favour of it (IR 3.15(1)).

Voting rights

9.17 A creditor is only entitled to vote at the meeting if:

(a)   he has given to the receiver, not later than 1200 hours on the business day before the date fixed for the meeting, details of the debt claimed due to him and the claim has been admitted (IR 3.11(1)(a)); and
(b)   there has been lodged with the administrative receiver prior to the meeting any proxy which the creditor intends to be used on his behalf (IR 3.11(1)(b)).

9.18 The chairman may allow the creditor to vote notwithstanding that he has failed to comply with paragraph 9.17(a) above, if satisfied that the failure was due to factors beyond the creditor's control (IR 3.11(2)).

9.19 A creditor cannot vote in respect of a debt for an unliquidated amount or any debt whose value is not ascertained except where the chairman agrees to put upon the debt an estimated minimum amount for voting purposes (IR 3.11(5)). A secured creditor can only vote in respect of the unsecured element of his debt, if any (IR 3.11(6)).

Admission and Rejection of Claims

9.20 The chairman can admit or reject all or a part of creditors' claims for the purposes of voting (IR 3.12(1)) but his decision can be subject to appeal to the court by any creditor (IR 3.12(2)). If the chairman is in doubt about the validity of a claim he must mark it as objected to and allow the creditor to vote, subject to the vote being subsequently invalid if the objection is sustained (IR 3.12(3)).

If on appeal the chairman's decision is overturned or a creditor's vote declared invalid the court may order that another meeting be summoned or make any other order as it thinks just (IR 3.12(4)). Neither the administrative receiver nor any person nominated by him to be chairman is personally liable for costs incurred by any person in respect of any appeal to the court, unless the court so orders (IR 3.12(5)).

Quorum

9.21 Obviously, no resolution can be put to the meeting unless a quorum is present. A quorum is three creditors present or represented, or the only or both the creditors if there are less than three (IR 3.13(1)). One person may constitute a quorum if he is the chairman or a creditor of the company and holds sufficient proxies to make up the number required (IR 3.13(2)).

There is no need to adjourn the meeting if there is no quorum present (IR 3.14).

The chairman is responsible for keeping a record of the meeting and these minutes are to be kept as part of the records of the receivership (IR 3.15(2)). They must include a list of the creditors who attended (either personally or by proxy) and if a creditors committee is formed (see paragraph 9.24 et seq below) the names and addresses of those elected to be members of that committee (IR 3.15(3)).

Group Companies

9.22 In the case of groups of companies it may be convenient to hold a joint meeting. In this case, however:

(a)   a separate report must be prepared for each company to which an administrative receiver has been appointed;

(b)   the appointment of committees must be handled on a company by company basis, although there is no objection to the same creditor(s) serving on more than one committee; and

(c)   whilst it will only be necessary to prepare one set of minutes, signed copies should be placed on the record files for each company and separate attendance lists should be maintained.

Liquidation

9.23 If:

(a)   the company goes into liquidation before the creditors' meeting is convened; and

(b)   the administrative receiver sends a copy of his report to the liquidator:

(i)   within seven days of sending it to the Registrar of Companies and the secured creditors (or within seven days of the liquidator's appointment, if later) (IA s 48(4)(a)), and

(ii)   within three months of his own appointment (IA s 48(4)(b));

he need not send copies to the unsecured creditors or hold a creditors meeting.

Creditors Committee

9.24 If a committee is established, the record of the meeting must include a list of the names and addresses of those elected to it (IR 3.15(3)).

The committee must consist of not less than three and not more than five creditors elected at the meeting (IR 3.16(1)). A body corporate may be appointed in its own name but can only act through a duly authorised representative.

9.25 The committee does not formally exist until the administrative receiver has issued a certificate of due constitution (IR 3.17(1)). The certificate can only be issued when three members have agreed to act (IR 3.17(2)) and when the others, if any, agree then an amended certificate must be issued (IR 3.17(3)).

The certificate and any amended certificates must be sent to the Registrar of Companies (see appendix H.5). (IR 3.17(4)). Any changes in the membership of the committee must be reported to the Registrar of Companies (see appendix H.6).

9.26 The function of the committee is to assist the administrative receiver in such manner as may be agreed from time to time (IR 3.18(1)). The first meeting of the committee is to be called within three months of its establishment and thereafter within 21 days of the administrative receiver having received a request by a member for a meeting (IR 3.18(3)(a)). A meeting is to be called also if a resolution has been passed that a meeting should be held on a particular date (IR 3.18(3)(b)). The administrative receiver must give seven days notice in writing of the venue to every member unless the requirement of notice has been waived (IR 3.28(4)).

9.27 The chairman at any meeting must be the administrative receiver or a person nominated in writing by him who may either be a person who is qualified to act as an insolvency practitioner in relation to the company or an employee of the administrative receiver who is sufficiently experienced (IR 3.19).

9.28 A quorum at any meeting is at least two members either present or represented (IR 3.20). A member may be represented by another person provided that person has a letter of authority signed by the committee member which entitles him to act (IR 3.21(1) and (2)).

The chairman may ask a representative to produce his letter of authority and exclude him if it appears deficient. No member may be represented by a body corporate, an undischarged bankrupt or a person subject to a composition or arrangement with his creditors (IR 3.21(4)).

No person can, on the same committee, act as a representative of more than one member nor can he act both as a member and another member's representative (IR 3.21(5)).

9.29 A member can resign by notice in writing delivered to the administrative receiver (IR 3.22). Membership is automatically terminated if a member:

(a) becomes bankrupt, or compounds or arranges with his creditors;
(b) at three consecutive meetings is neither present nor represented (unless at the third meeting this rule is resolved not to apply);
(c) ceases to be, or is found never to have been, a creditor.
 (IR 3.23(1)).

If the cause of termination is the member's bankruptcy then his trustee in bankruptcy replaces him on the committee (IR 3.23(2)).

9.30 A member may be removed by resolution of a meeting of creditors at least fourteen days notice having been given of the proposed resolution (IR 3.24).

9.31 If a vacancy arises, it need not be filled if the administrative receiver and a majority of those remaining so agree, provided the number of members does not fall below three. Any creditor may be appointed by the receiver to fill the vacancy if a majority of the other members agree to the appointment and the creditor consents to act (IR 3.25).

9.32 At any meeting each member has one vote and a resolution is passed when a majority present or represented have voted in favour of it. Every resolution passed shall be recorded and the record signed by the chairman and kept as part of the receivership records (IR 3.26).

9.33 The administrative receiver may wish to obtain the members' agreement to a resolution by post (IR 3.27(1)).

If so he must send out to members (or their representatives as the case may be) a statement incorporating the resolution, each resolution (if more than one) being sent out in a separate document (IR 3.27(2)). Any member may, within seven days of the sending out of the resolution, require the administrative receiver to summon a meeting to consider the matters raised by the resolution (IR 3.27(3)). In the absence of such a request the resolution is deemed to have been passed when the administrative receiver has been notified by a majority of the members that they concur with it (IR 3.27(4)).

Information from Administrative Receiver

9.34 Where the committee resolves to require the attendance of the administrative receiver under Section 49(2), the notice must be signed by the majority of the members (IR 3.28(1)) and sent to him giving not less than seven days notice of the business day fixed for the meeting. The administrative receiver can hold the meeting at such time and place as he determines (IR 3.28(2)). At this meeting the committee may elect a member to be chairman in place of the administrative receiver or his nominee. The administrative receiver must furnish the committee with such information relating to the carrying out of his functions as is reasonable.

Expenses of Committee Members

9.35 The reasonable travelling expenses of members or their representatives incurred in travelling to attend committee meetings or otherwise on the committee's business can be paid as an expense of the receivership (IR 3.29(1)). Expenses relating to attendance at any meeting held within three months of the previous one are not refundable unless the meeting is called on the initiative of the administrative receiver (IR 3.29(2)).

9.36 Members may deal with the company while the administrative receiver is acting, provided that any transactions are for value and in good faith (IR 3.30(1)). On the application of any interested person the court may set aside any transaction which appears not to be so and may give directions for compensating the company for any loss it may have suffered as a result of the transaction (IR 3.30(2)).

Reports on Directors

9.37 The Insolvent Companies (Reports on Conduct of Directors) (No.2) Rules 1986 place on every administrative receiver appointed on or after 29 December 1986 a statutory duty to submit to the Department of Trade and Industry within six months of the relevant date reports and/or returns covering all those who were directors or shadow directors of the company at any time within the three years preceding the insolvency, the relevant date being the date of appointment.

Duty to Report

9.38 These Rules, and Section 7(3) of the Company Directors Disqualification Act 1986, impose on an administrative receiver a duty to *report* to the Secretary of State for Trade and Industry if he forms the view that the conduct of a director or former director makes him unfit to be concerned in the management of a company. Directors for this purpose include shadow directors. The forms to be used (D2, D2(A), D2(B) and D5) are prescribed by the Rules (see appendices H.16-H.19).

9.39 Whilst it is the administrative receiver's responsibility to submit a report if he considers one or more directors unfit to be concerned in the management of a company, the Secretary of State is responsible for deciding whether or not to apply to the court for a disqualification order.

Duty to Submit a Return

9.40 Within six months of the appointment, unless he has reported on *every* person who was a director or shadow director within the three years preceding the insolvency, the administrative receiver must submit a *return* to the Secretary of State. The return must include a complete list of those who were directors or shadow directors within the three years and indicate whether the reason for not submitting reports on them is that:

(a) the company is in fact in a position to pay all its liabilities and the costs of any winding up in full;
(b) the administrative receiver has not become aware of any matter which would require him to submit a report (i.e. any evidence of unfitness to be concerned in the management of a company within the meaning of the statute); or
(c) he has insufficient information.

Any return must be submitted on form D5 (see appendix H.19).

9.41 An administrative receiver who fails to submit a return when under a duty to do so is liable to a fine not exceeding £400 plus a £40 daily default fine. Where the administrative receiver forms the view that one or more directors is or are unfit to be concerned in the management of a company, he must submit a report to that effect even if he has previously stated that he has no reason to believe that director or those directors to be unfit.

Duty to Provide Information

9.42 Under Section 7(4) of the Company Directors Disqualification Act 1986 the Secretary of State may require the administrative receiver:

(a) to furnish him with information regarding any person's conduct as a director of the company; and
(b) to produce and permit inspection of books, papers and other records relevant to that person's conduct as director.

DTI Guidance Notes

9.43 The Department of Trade and Industry's guidance notes give very useful guidance on the questions that should be considered when completing the D forms and the extent of the information that should be supplied if it does appear that a director is unfit to be concerned in the management of a company.

9.44 The guidance notes specifically state that the administrative receiver 'is not obliged to undertake investigations which he would not otherwise have considered it necessary to make'. They also make it clear that directors should not be regarded as unfit simply because of relatively insignificant breaches of statutory duties.

Identification of Directors

9.45 It is considered that the administrative receiver should take reasonable steps to identify those who were directors at any time within the three years. As a minimum the file at the Companies Registration Office should be searched and the company's minute book and register of directors inspected.

9.46 There is no need to investigate the possibility that the company had shadow directors unless in the course of his work the administrative receiver becomes aware that this may have been the case. If the minutes reveal that someone who was not a director of the company was in regular attendance at board meetings, enquiries should be made regarding his function within the company (even if he held an office, such as that of company secretary, which obviously required his attendance at board meetings; in practice he may have participated in policy decisions). A parent company may be a shadow director of its subsidiary if the subsidiary's directors are accustomed to act in accordance with its directions or instructions (IA s 251).

9.47 If there is any doubt as to whether a particular person was a director or shadow director during the relevant period, it should be assumed that he *was*; the reason for the doubt should be mentioned in the report to the Secretary of State.

Preparation of Report

9.48 Having identified the directors and/or shadow directors, these names must be entered on the form D2 together with the relevant details of the company as required by the form. A separate form D2(A) has also to be submitted which provides further information on the company.

If the administrative receiver has formed a view that one or more of those persons listed on the form D2 is or are considered to be unfit to be concerned in the management of a company then a separate form D2(B) must be completed for each person(s). He will have indicated on form D2 that he has formed this view by making a 'Y' against the relevant name(s) in the appropriate column of page 2.

When completing the form D2(B), if it is necessary, the receiver should take into account information normally available to him and it is not necessary to undertake any additional investigations or enquiries.

More than One Administrative Receiver

9.49 In the case of joint appointments, each appointee has a duty to ensure that a report or interim return is submitted. When a company goes into liquidation after the appointment of an administrative receiver, both the administrative receiver and the liquidator have a duty to submit a report or return (the liquidator may have to investigate matters which do not affect the administrative receiver and have therefore not been considered by him).

9.50 When an appointment is accepted jointly with a partner from another firm both should sign the report or return.

Group and Connected Companies

9.51 If companies in the same group have administrative receivers appointed at the same time, a separate duty to report or submit returns arises in respect of each one. All reports and returns should be submitted to the Secretary of State at the same time, as far as possible.

VAT Bad Debt Relief Certificates

9.52 As soon as an administrative receiver forms the view that if the company went into liquidation the assets would be insufficient to cover the payment of any dividend in respect of debts which are neither preferential nor secured then he must issue a certificate of insolvency in the terms of the Value Added Tax Act 1983, s 22(3)(b) (see appendix I.8). (IR 3.36). The certificate must be placed with the company's records and all creditors known to have made taxable supplies notified of its issue within two months or within three months of the administrative receiver's appointment, whichever is the later (IR 3.37).

9.53 Until such time as the position becomes clear or a liquidator is appointed, the possibility of a dividend being paid on ordinary unsecured claims in the event of a liquidation should be considered:

(a)   immediately upon appointment;
(b)   each time a report is sent to the debenture holder;
(c)   when the statement of affairs is received from the directors; and
(d)   three months after appointment.

Chapter 10

Other Matters

10.1　This chapter considers other matters of concern to the administrative receiver:

(a)　The remuneration of the administrative receiver.
(b)　Abstract of receipts and payments.
(c)　Vacation of office.
(d)　The termination of the receivership.

Remuneration

10.2　Generally the remuneration of the administrative receiver is agreed with the debenture holder and takes into account the responsibility and complexity of the work to be carried out. His remuneration ranks ahead of the preferential creditors and, if he has vacated office on the making of an administration order, he is entitled to be paid his remuneration and any expenses properly incurred by him out of any property of the company which had been under his control in priority to any security held by his appointor (IA s 11(4)).

10.3　A liquidator may apply to the court for an order to fix the remuneration of the administrative receiver and this can be in respect of the period prior to the application to the court (IA s 36(1)). Following an order under Section 36(1) the liquidator or administrative receiver can apply to the court for a variation to that order from time to time (IA s 36(3)).

Abstract of Receipts and Payments

10.4　The administrative receiver must, within two months of the end of the twelve months following his appointment, within two months of every subsequent period of twelve months, and within two months after he ceased to act, send a copy of his receipts and payments to the following (IR 3.32):

(a)　the Registrar of Companies;
(b)　the company;
(c)　his appointor;
(d)　each member of the creditors committee (if there is one).

10.5　The administrative receiver may apply to the court to extend the period of two months referred to in paragraph 10.4.

10.6　The abstract of his receipts and payments is to be submitted on form 3.6 (see appendix H.7). The obligation on the administrative receiver to submit this does not remove the duty on him to maintain proper books of account and render proper accounts otherwise than above.

Vacation of Office

10.7　The office can be vacated in the following circumstances:

(a)　removed by order of the court (IA s 45(1));
(b)　resignation;

(c)   death;
(d)   office holder ceased to be qualified to act as an insolvency practitioner (IA s 45(2));
(e)   vacation on completion of the receivership.

10.8   At any time that an administrative receiver vacates office, he is entitled to receive his remuneration and expenses properly incurred and any indemnity to which he is entitled from the property of the company under his control in priority to any security held by his appointor (IA s 45(3)).

10.9   Where an administrative receiver vacates office otherwise than by death he must, within fourteen days, send a notice to that effect to the registrar of companies on form No.405(2). (See appendix H.14). (IA s 45(4) and CA s 405(2)).

Resignation

10.10   Before resigning his office the administrative receiver must give at least seven days notice of his intention to do so to (IR 3.33(1)):

(a)   his appointor;
(b)   the company or if it is in liquidation, the liquidator.

The notice [form 3.9] (see appendix H.10) must specify the date on which the resignation is to take effect (IR 3.33(2)). No notice is necessary if the resignation follows the making of an administration order.

Death

10.11   If the administrative receiver dies, his appointor must immediately give notice on form 3.7 (see appendix H.8) (IR 3.34) to:

(a)   the Registrar of Companies;
(b)   the company or if it is in liquidation, the liquidator.

Vacation on Completion of Receivership or on Ceasing to be Qualified as an Insolvency Practitioner

10.12   On either of these two circumstances arising the administrative receiver must immediately notify:

(a)   if the company is in liquidation, the liquidator;
(b)   in any case, the members of the creditors committee (if any) (IR 3.35(1));
(c)   the Registrar of Companies by means of an endorsement on the notice submitted under paragraph 10.9 above (IA s 45(4) and IR 3.35(2)).

The Termination of the Receivership

10.13   The order of application of money in the hands of the administrative receiver will usually be as follows:

(a)   The costs of realisation of the company's property.
(b)   The outgoings and costs incurred by the receiver in carrying on the business and in collecting and recovering the company's assets.
(c)   The receiver's remuneration.
(d)   The payment to the debenture holder of net monies arising from assets subject to the fixed charge. (See paragraph 10.14 below.)
(e)   The preferential creditors.
(f)   The balance of interest due under the debenture (subject to the terms of the debenture).
(g)   The balance of the principal sum secured by the debenture.

10.14   A fixed charge must be repaid from the realisation of assets covered by that charge, subject only to the costs of realisation, which include the receiver's remuneration. It is important to note however that following the decision in *Re G L Saunders Ltd* [1986] 1 WLR 215 any surplus available under a fixed charge is not subject to a floating charge held by the same creditor. A receiver must therefore pay any such surplus to the company or liquidator if the company is in liquidation or to any subsequent chargeholder.

10.15 In addition to the monies owing on the debenture, the receiver will normally pay legal charges incurred by and, if applicable, remuneration of the debenture holder or trustee for the debenture holder, as these items are mortgagee's expenses and may be added to the security under the terms of most charges.

10.16 It is not unusual to make payments on account to the debenture holder, but the receiver must ensure that he has sufficient funds in hand to meet all prior costs and expenses, including his remuneration and, in the case of a floating charge, the claims of the preferential creditors.

10.17 If, at the end of the receivership, there are unrealised assets and/or liquid funds in the receiver's hands in excess of the amount due under the debenture, the surplus must either be returned to the company or be passed to the liquidator, if one has been appointed. If the surplus is returned to the company when it is still trading, the receiver should protect himself against possible claims by obtaining an indemnity from the company, supported by suitable security to the extent of available assets. If the surplus is passed to a liquidator the receiver should make an arrangement with the liquidator whereby the receiver retains some of his realisations or control over them for a period of at least a year after he ceased trading, as a protection against possible claims. He should also endeavour to obtain an indemnity from the liquidator which, in practice, will be limited to the value of assets remaining in the liquidator's possession.

10.18 If there is a second charge ranking after the receiver's charge, the second chargee will usually be entitled to the receiver's surplus in priority to the company or liquidator. In these circumstances, the receiver should obtain the written agreement of the company, or liquidator, and of the second chargee as to the manner in which he disposes of the surplus. If the receiver is unable to obtain such agreement, he should take legal advice.

10.19 The receiver should also endeavour to protect his position by seeking written confirmation from firms with which he has dealt, to the effect that they have no further claims against him.

10.20 It is a shortcoming of the Insolvency Act that it contains no provisions whereby receivers can protect themselves against preferential or other claims received after they have disposed of the assets in their hands. Where the receiver is appointed by a bank, the original indemnity obtained by him on his appointment should be worded to cover him against claims after the termination of his receivership. If the receiver has been unable to obtain such an indemnity, considerable care should be taken before surplus assets are handed back to the company.

10.21 If the administrative receiver vacates office prior to completion of the receivership he is still obliged to discharge the liabilities set out in 10.13 (a), (b), (c) and (e) above. He is entitled to an indemnity, charged on and payable out of any property which was under his custody and control in priority to his appointor, in respect of any of the above liabilities. The only circumstance where he does not have to pay the preferential creditors (10.13(e) above) arises where he vacates office on the making of an administration order (IA s 11(5)).

10.22 Finally, before vacating office on completion of the receivership, the consent to the filing of the notice of ceasing to act (see paragraph 10.8 above) should be obtained from the appointor although he will have received notice under paragraph 10.10 above.

Chapter 11

Conclusion

11.1   It is appropriate to end this manual with a summary of the pros and cons of administrative receivership from the viewpoints of the lender and the various institutions and government agencies which are concerned with the health of the corporate sector. Inevitably, by reviewing the subject in this way, we are repeating much of what has gone before in this manual, but we believe, nonetheless, that it is useful to have such a 'reprise' to provide a quick general survey of the subject for those occasions when readers have insufficient time to study the detailed considerations.

Advantages of Receivership

11.2   Receivership has advantages as a means of rescuing the viable parts of companies in difficulties because:

(a)   The appointment of an administrative receiver frees a business from the burden of its existing debts and in that way gives it the opportunity for a fresh start.

(b)   The administrative receiver has greater powers to continue trading than a liquidator, although he will only do so if he has good reason to believe that his actions will increase the ultimate disposal proceeds and will not worsen the position of the general creditors.

(c)   When the company has a complex structure or a wide range of products, an administrative receiver may be able to disentangle the profitable activities and elements from the remaining part of the business. The viable elements can then continue under the umbrella of a new company, or be sold to other companies as going concerns.

(d)   Despite the fact that they will not receive payment of their past debts, the administrative recciver's dealings with trade creditors can often be relatively harmonious. If they co-operate, they may share in an increased realisation, and they can also hope to retain an outlet for their products through the new company.

(e)   Customers can also be in a similar situation. They may find that they cannot obtain the products they need from another supplier without costly delays. It is therefore in their best interests to co-operate with the administrative receiver in seeking the continuation of the business even if they have lost payments on account already made or the administrative receiver has increased the price of the company's products.

(f)   Reduction of the labour force and improvements in productivity can sometimes be more easily achieved by an administrative receiver than otherwise since the stark alternative can be clearly seen.

11.3   Two words of warning should be sounded here. First, a business which has been failing under existing management is unlikely to be turned around quickly under a receivership, particularly as morale will be at a low level and experienced management will probably be in the process of drifting away in search of new career opportunities. Continued trading by an administrative receiver should therefore generally be looked at as a bridging operation lasting for a few weeks, while attempts are made to attract a buyer of the business as a going concern. Second, if a buyer of the business is to be successful, he must have adequate financial resources both to meet the purchase price and to provide whatever additional working capital may be needed. He must also have the management resources which will be able to cope with the heavy demands such an exercise entails.

Some Disadvantages of Receivership

11.4   Whilst receivership can be an effective means of sifting and preserving the viable activities of companies in financial difficulties, certain hazards exist for anyone who is contemplating using receivership as a route to rescue:

(a)   An administrative receivership appointment may not be legally possible as there may not be any debenture holder. Even if one exists, either the amount involved may be relatively small or the necessary floating charge may have been taken so recently that the bank will be inhibited by legal constraints from appointing an administrative receiver.

(b)   An administration order may be in force, which precludes the appointment of an administrative receiver.

(c)   The administrative receiver may not wish to take on the risks associated with continued trading. He may wish to press ahead with closures, and at the very least will seek to be fully indemnified against any potential claims which would arise if he continues to trade.

(d)   There may not be any willing purchasers for the constituent parts of a business, especially in times of economic recession.

(e)   Receiverships may have a damaging effect on sub-contractors, and suppliers. When a company or its viable parts are salvaged through receivership, the old company usually goes into liquidation. This means that the old company's creditors may only receive a part of the monies due to them.

(f)   Where existing contracts contain a clause permitting cancellation by one party if the other goes into receivership the business might lose valuable orders or find itself faced with more onerous conditions imposed by suppliers.

(g)   The credibility of the company may be damaged beyond repair, particularly overseas where administrative receivers are often confused with liquidators.

(h)   Foreign creditors of a UK company which goes into receivership may seize that company's overseas assets as security against the debts owed to them.

Receivership v Administration Order

11.5   It is appropriate before finally concluding to draw attention very briefly to the main differences between receiverships and administration orders, to which reference in this manual has been made from time to time.

Whilst the administration order procedure will be described in great detail in a companion volume to this manual, it is important to identify the main differences between this and the administrative receiver.

The circumstances under which an administration order will be made are generally going to occur when a company is in financial difficulty but there is no body holding a floating charge and thus capable of appointing an administrative receiver. It is likely that lenders such as the joint stock banks will, whenever possible, take floating charges and thus be able to appoint a receiver whose functions have been considered in detail in this manual. If however there is no floating charge the directors, normally, or the creditors may petition for an administration order. The effect of this is that if the order is made no secured creditor can enforce his security and that includes any person holding either a fixed or floating charge, a lien, retention of title or rights under a hire purchase agreement. The administrator is in office in order to put in place proposals which will be of greater benefit to the general body of creditors, both secured and unsecured, than would be the case in liquidation. The powers of the administrator are generally similar to the administrative receiver but he has greater powers in relation to the prevention of secured creditors exercising their rights. The administrative receiver has a statutory duty to deal with the preferential creditors whereas the administrator has no such duty.

It is fundamental that any person capable of appointing an administrative receiver acts quickly in making a decision on whether to appoint as he will have only a five day period from receipt of the petition for the order and the hearing of the order. Thereafter, whilst the administrator is in office, an administrative receiver cannot be appointed.

Appendices, Official Forms, Specimen Forms, Receivership Letters and Receivership Instructions and Memoranda

Appendix A

Receivership Check List

Name of company ....

Number of company ....

Registered office ....

Name(s) of administrative receiver(s) ....

Date of appointment ....

Name of appointor ....

Manual Reference		Matters to be dealt with	Initials and date

Statutory matters

Immediate action

3.11	1	Accept appointment before end of the business day following the date of receipt of the deed of appointment (see appendix I.1). (Joint appointees must accept on their own behalf. Appointment is only effective when all appointees have accepted and is deemed to be effective from the date the deed of appointment was received.)	
3.12	2	Each appointee to confirm acceptance of the appointment in writing. The confirmation can be by a person duly authorised to do so and it must state: (a) The time and date of receipt of notice of the appointment. (b) The time and date of the acceptance (see 1 above).	
9.2	3	Send a notice of appointment to the company (see appendix I.2).	
3.13	4	Ensure that the notice of appointment (form 405[1]) is filed at Companies House within 7 days. [This is the responsibility of the appointor.] (See appendix H.13.)	
9.3	5	Advertise the appointment once in the Gazette and once in an appropriate newspaper (see appendix I.4).	
9.5	6	Send a letter and form 3.1 to all those required to submit a statement of affairs (see appendix J.1).	
2.3	7	Obtain a 'certificate of specific penalty' under bonding arrangements.	

Manual Reference		Matters to be dealt with	Initials and date
2.4	8	Open 'Statutory Record' (see appendix H.1).	
4.16	9	Ensure that a notice stating that joint administrative receivers have been appointed appears on all company correspondence, orders and invoices.	
		Within 28 days	
9.4	10	Send a copy of the notice of appointment to all creditors (see appendix I.3).	
		Within 3 months	
9.12 et seq	11	Send a copy of the statutory report to the following: (a) The registrar of companies (form 3.10) (see appendix H.11). (b) Any trustees for secured creditors. (c) The secured creditors. The copy being sent to the registrar must have attached to it a copy of the statement of affairs (form 3.2) and copies of any statements of concurrence (see appendix H.3).	
9.23	12	If a liquidator has been appointed then, within 7 days of complying with 11 above, send a copy of the report to the liquidator.	
9.13	13	*If no liquidator appointed*: either, send a copy of the report to all creditors, or publish a notice in the newspaper (see 5 above) stating an address to which unsecured creditors should write for a free copy of the report (see appendix I.7).	
9.12 et seq	14	*If no liquidator appointed*: call a meeting of the unsecured creditors giving not less than 14 days notice.	
9.24	15	If at the meeting of unsecured creditors a creditors committee is formed, then issue a certificate of due constitution and forward it to the registrar of companies (form 3.4) (see appendix H.5).	
9.23	16	*If a liquidator has been appointed prior to the convening of the meeting of unsecured creditors* then the meeting of unsecured creditors (see 14 et seq) need not be held.	
9.13	17	If the statement of affairs was not available for forwarding to the registrar with the report send it as soon as it is available (form 3.3) (see appendix H.4).	
		After 3 months	
9.26	18	Call a meeting of the creditors committee within 3 months of its establishment.	
		Within 6 months	
9.37 et seq	19	Submit reports or returns on conduct of directors.	

Manual Reference		Matters to be dealt with	Initials and date
		For regular review	
9.25	20	If any change occurs to the membership of the committee report the change to the registrar of companies (form 3.5) (see appendix H.6).	
7.10 et seq	21	If an order has been made by the Court which sanctioned the disposal of charged property then a notice must be sent to the registrar of companies within 14 days (form 3.8), together with an office copy of the order (see appendix H.9).	
10.4 et seq	22	Within 2 months after the end of the first 12 months and thereafter every 12 months, send an abstract of receipts and payments (form 3.6) to: the registrar of companies the company his appointor each member of the creditors committee (see appendix H.7).	
9.52	23	Consider whether a VAT bad debt relief certificate should be issued (see appendix I.8).	
		Prior to completion	
10.2	24	When sufficient assets have been realised and all costs have been paid, agree the receiver's remuneration with the debenture holder.	
10.13 et seq	25	Having obtained tax clearance, make distributions in the following order: (a) To any debenture holders holding a fixed charge. (b) Preferential creditors. (c) To debenture holder under floating charge. (d) The surplus is to be handed over to the company or to the liquidator should one have been appointed (or to a second chargee).	
10.22	26	Obtain a release from the debenture holder.	
		On completion	
10.9	27	Immediately on ceasing to act send a notice (form 405[2]) to the registrar of companies (see appendix H.14).	
10.4	28	Within 2 months of ceasing to act send an abstract of receipts and payments for the period since the previous abstract to those per para 22 above.	

Appendix B

Receivership Check List

Name of company ....

Number of company ....

Registered office ....

Name(s) of administrative receiver(s) ....

Date of appointment ....

Name of appointor ....

Manual Reference		Matters to be dealt with	Initials and date
		Administration	
3.14	1	Obtain legal advice on the validity of the appointment.	
	2	Immobilize any document shredder(s) on the premises.	
4.3 et seq	3	Meet the directors and senior management to advise them of the appointment and of the legal and practical consequences.	
4.5	4	Consider what immediate instructions are needed with regard to deliveries inwards and outwards, with particular attention to:	
		(a) Transport companies who are owed money and whom the receiver may wish to employ (see appendix J.19).	
		(b) Customers with credit balances where the receiver wishes to make future deliveries (see appendix J.20).	
		(c) Customers' ability to pay.	
		(d) Goods subject to reserved title.	
4.5	5	Arrange for physical stock check.	
4.6	6	Ensure staff are instructed that they may not enter into any commitments without the sanction of the receiver.	
4.7	7	Take charge of cheque books and credit cards.	
4.8	8	Inform company's banks by telephone followed by letter (see appendix J.6), or telex.	
4.10 et seq	9	Ascertain from the company's chief accountant:	
		(a) Immediate cash requirements and anticipated cash flow.	

Manual Reference		Matters to be dealt with	Initials and date
	(b)	Whether it is necessary to borrow.	
	(c)	Where immediate economies can be made.	
4.14	10	Ensure that there is adequate and effective insurance cover.	
4.15	11	Give instructions that all incoming and outgoing mail is to be seen by the receiver.	
4.16	12	Order rubber stamps and, if necessary, printed documents so that all stationery used by the company has the words 'Receiver (or Administrative Receiver) appointed on . . . . . ' after the company's name.	
4.17	13	Instruct the company's chief accountant or other responsible official to provide schedules of assets showing each case (where applicable) which are the subject of retention of title clauses, hire purchase contracts, charges or garnishee orders. The schedules should also show, where applicable, approximate book values and estimated realisable values.	
		In practice, this work may have to be undertaken at least in part by the receiver and his staff.	
4.17	14	Obtain from agents and incorporate in above schedules, valuations of all fixed assets and stock.	
4.19	15	Talk to employees or their representatives.	
4.20	16	Advise Department of Employment and any recognised trade union of impending redundancies, and possible transfer of undertaking (see appendices J.13 and J.12).	
4.20	17	Obtain forms and booklets for the operation of the insolvency provisions of EPCA 78.	
6.26	18	Consider whether the business should be hived-down.	
4.13	19	Carry out search of file at Companies House.	
4.24	20	Consider action to be taken regarding employees.	
	21	Write in accordance with standard letters adjusted to suit particular circumstances: See appendices J.1 – J.35.	
	22	Send out instructions adjusted to suit particular circumstances: See appendices K.1 – K.10.	
	23	A master file must be kept for each receivership. It should contain the following information:	
		(a) A copy of the debenture holder's charge.	
		(b) A copy of the deed of appointment.	
		(c) Notes of meetings with debenture holders.	
		(d) Notes of meetings with officials of the company.	
		(e) Notes of meetings with creditors.	
		(f) Notes recording the broad progress of the assignment.	

Manual Reference		Matters to be dealt with	Initials and date
		(g) Reasons for major policy decisions.	
		(h) Copies of all accounts filed by the receiver.	
		(i) Copy of the summary of the statement of affairs and receiver's comments.	
		(j) Notes of periodic reviews of the receivership by the partner in charge.	
		(k) Statutory record (see appendix A, paragraph 8).	
5.5	24	Open receivership cash book to record all receipts and payments.	
5.13 et seq	25	Scrutinise all contracts and take appropriate action.	
8.6	26	Scrutinise all leases and take appropriate action.	
5.24	27	Consider the requirements of the licensing provisions of the Consumer Credit Act 1974 and ensure that, wherever necessary, the company or the receiver, as the case may be, holds an appropriate current licence in relation to continuation of the business or collection or compromise of book debts covered by the Act.	
5.77(a)	28	Ascertain whether any patented processes or other industrial rights are used under licence to ensure that the terms of the licence are complied with.	
5.77(b)	29	Ascertain whether any of the company's activities or products are likely to infringe patents or other industrial rights of a third party. Legal advice should be taken if this appears to be the case.	
5.13 et seq	30	Ensure that any amendments to the company's purchase and sale contracts which the receiver considers necessary are communicated to the supplier or customer concerned before further deliveries are accepted or made.	
	31	Books and papers: (a) Ensure security of statutory books and seal. (b) Obtain a list of the company's books and records. (c) Obtain a list of the company's documents of title.	
	32	Arrange for redirection of correspondence if necessary.	
5.98 et seq	33	Arrange for a review of the taxation position of the company. Ensure that any necessary appeals or returns requiring urgent attention are dealt with.	
5.67 et seq	34	Examine company pension scheme (if any).	

Appendix C

Powers of Administrative Receiver
(As Schedule 1 Insolvency Act 1986)

1   Power to take possession of, collect and get in the property of the company and, for that purpose, to take such proceedings as may seem to him expedient.

2   Power to sell or otherwise dispose of the property of the company by public auction or private contract or, in Scotland, to sell, feu, hire out or otherwise dispose of the property of the company by public roup or private bargain.

3   Power to raise or borrow money and grant security therefor over the property of the company.

4   Power to appoint a solicitor or accountant or other professionally qualified person to assist him in the performance of his functions.

5   Power to bring or defend any action or other legal proceedings in the name and on behalf of the company.

6   Power to refer to arbitration any question affecting the company.

7   Power to effect and maintain insurances in respect of the business and property of the company.

8   Power to use the company's seal.

9   Power to do all acts and to execute in the name and on behalf of the company any deed, receipt or other document.

10   Power to draw, accept, make and endorse any bill of exchange or promissory note in the name and on behalf of the company.

11   Power to appoint any agent to do any business which he is unable to do himself or which can more conveniently be done by an agent and power to employ and dismiss employees.

12   Power to do all such things (including the carrying out of works) as may be necessary for the realisation of the property of the company.

13   Power to make any payment which is necessary or incidental to the performance of his functions.

14   Power to carry on the business of the company.

15   Power to establish subsidiaries of the company.

16   Power to transfer to subsidiaries of the company the whole or any part of the business and property of the company.

17   Power to grant or accept a surrender of a lease or tenancy of any of the property of the company, and to take a lease or tenancy of any property required or convenient for the business of the company.

18   Power to make any arrangement or compromise on behalf of the company.

19   Power to call up any uncalled capital of the company.

20   Power to rank and claim in the bankruptcy, insolvency, sequestration or liquidation of any person indebted to the company and to receive dividends, and to accede to trust deeds for the creditors of any such person.

21   Power to present or defend a petition for the winding up of the company.

22   Power to change the situation of the company's registered office.

23   Power to do all other things incidental to the exercise of the foregoing powers.

Pro Forma Financial Position as at 31 December 1986

	Per Audited Accounts 31 March 1986		Approximate Book Values 31 December 1986		Estimated Realisable Values 'Going Concern' Basis		'Forced Sale' Basis	
	£'000	£'000	£'000	£'000	£'000	£'000	£'000	£'000
Assets subject to fixed charge:								
Freehold factory and offices	124		128		293		203	
Less: 1st mortgage	51		50		50		50	
	73		78		243		153	
Trade and sundry debtors	502		550		500		340	
Investments in subsidiaries	27		3		—		—	
	602		631		743		493	
	296		521		521		521	
Deduct: Secured by fixed charge		306		110		222		(28)
Assets subject to the bank's floating charge:								
Plant, machinery and equipment	130		96		83		25	
Stocks (after providing for reservation of title claims)	590		404		400		75	
Prepaid expenditure	34		11		10		—	
	754		511		493		100	
Preferential and priority creditors:								
PAYE, NIC, VAT, wages, holiday pay, etc.	38		49		50		50	
	716		462		443		50	
	1022		572		665		22	
Debenture holder:								
Loan	63		63		63		63	
Overdraft, accrued interest and charges	233		458		458		458	
	296		521		521		521	
	296		521		521		521	
Less: Fixed charge security deducted above	—		—		—		—	
Unsecured creditors:								
Outstanding cheques	56		108		108		108	
Bills payable	17		57		57		57	
Trade and expense (after provision for reservation of title claims)	135		49		49		49	
	208		214		214		214	
Net assets		814		358		451		(192)
Issued share capital	262		262					
Share premium and reserves	552		96					
		814		358				

Notes: (1) The above estimates are subject to costs of realisation.
(2) There are contingent liabilities in respect of leasing agreements and for redundancies which have not been taken into account.

Appendix E

Preferential Creditors

1   The Insolvency Act 1986, Section 40 entitles certain creditors to receive payment of their debts subject to certain limitations in priority to the holder of a charge which, as created, was a floating charge. The preferential creditors are set out in Schedule 6 to the Act and are the amounts due at the relevant date being the date of appointment of the administrative receiver. (IA s 387(4)).

Broadly, the claims qualifying for preferential treatment are:

(a)   PAYE.
(b)   Social security contributions.
(c)   Occupational pension scheme contributions.
(d)   VAT.
(e)   Employees' arrears of earnings and holiday pay.
(f)   Miscellaneous taxes and duties.

2   PAYE

Amounts that have been or should have been deducted from wages and salaries *paid* in the twelve months preceding the relevant date. Amounts deducted from payments to sub-contractors in the construction industry during the same period are also preferential.

3   Social Security Contributions

Class 1 and Class 2 contributions due in respect of the twelve months preceding the relevant date.

4   Occupational Pension Scheme Contributions

Employees' contributions deducted from payments made in the four months preceding the relevant date but not paid to the pension scheme.

Employees' contributions to a contracted-out scheme are preferential to the extent of the sum needed to provide the minimum benefits under the scheme in relation to wages and salary paid or payable in respect of the twelve months preceding the relevant date. Where this cannot be identified, it is to be taken as 7% of relevant earnings in the case of a non-contributory scheme and 4.5% in the case of a contributory scheme.

5   VAT

Value added tax due in respect of the six months preceding the relevant date.

6 Employees' arrears of earnings and holiday pay

(a) Employees (including part time employees) are able to claim preferentially for arrears of wages or salary becoming due during the four months before the receiver's appointment up to a maximum of £800.

(b) Where any payment has been made for such wages or salaries out of funds advanced for those purposes, the party (usually a bank) who has advanced the funds becomes a preferential creditor to the extent that claims that would have been preferential have been reduced thereby.

(c) The normal meaning of 'wages' is extended by EPCA Section 121(2) to include:
   (i) a guarantee payment (EPCA Section 12);
   (ii) remuneration on suspension on medical grounds for a period not exceeding twenty-six weeks;
   (iii) any payment for time off to carry out trade union activities or, in the case of employees who have been given notice of dismissal by reason of redundancy, to look for new employment or make arrangements for training for future employment; and
   (iv) remuneration under a protective award.

(d) Employees are also entitled to claim preferentially for accrued holiday pay due on termination of employment.

(e) Such a claim is preferential whether employment was terminated before or as a result of the receivership. Note that the principle of subrogation, as outlined in paragraph 6(b) above, applies where advances have been made in respect of accrued holiday pay.

(f) Payment during leave taken at the end of a period of overseas employment may not be preferential.

(g) Broadly speaking, there must be a contract of service (written, oral or implied) between a creditor and the company for a claim to be preferential. Claims which may create difficulty are:

   (i) *Commission*
   When an employee receives wages or salary wholly or in part by way of commission he must be entitled to treat such commission as wages or salary for preferential purposes.

   (ii) *Directors and Secretaries*
   Directors' fees are not preferential (*Re Newspaper Proprietary Syndicate* [1900] 2 Ch 349). If the director is an employee as well as a director, i.e. an executive director, the remuneration of such an executive is generally treated as preferential up to the statutory limit although there is some authority for excluding such claims. When the secretary is another company or an outside accountant then the fees would not be preferential since neither is regarded as an employee.

   (iii) *Contractors*
   Contractors' claims are only preferential if the contractor is really an employee, which is a very rare occurrence. However, there is much case law on the subject. One test is the extent of the control exercised by the employer. Legal advice should be sought in such circumstances. Check to see if he is VAT registered.

7 Miscellaneous Taxes and Duties

The following taxes and duties are preferential to the extent that they arose during the twelve months preceding the relevant date:

Car tax
General betting duty
Bingo duty
Pool betting duty
Gaming licence duty.

Appendix F

Amounts payable by the Secretary of State for Employment under the Insolvency Provisions of the Employment Protection (Consolidation) Act 1978

Payable to Employees

	Maximum amount	*Maximum period*	*Section of the Act*
Arrears of pay	£158 per week	8 weeks	122(3)(a)
Holiday pay in respect of the twelve months immediately preceding the relevant date including pay for accrued holidays and pay for holidays taken but for which no payment has been made by the employer	£158 per week	6 weeks	122(3)(c) 127(3)(a) 127(3)(b)
Pay in lieu of notice	£158 per week after mitigation and notional tax	12 weeks	49 122(3)(b)
Basic award of compensation for unfair dismissal	£158 per week		122(3)(d)

Notes:

1 The insolvency provisions do not apply to certain classes of employee, in particular where under a contract of employment the employee ordinarily works outside the European Community (Insolvency of Employer (Excluded Classes) Regulations 1983 (SI 1983 No 624)).

2 The amounts concerned are those due to the employee at the 'relevant date' (EPCA 78 Section 122(2)) which is defined as the later of:

(a) the date of the receiver's appointment or the date on which the company went into liquidation (if earlier) (EPCA 78 Section 127(1)(c));
(b) the date the employee's employment terminated.

Claims should be calculated in accordance with the normal principles applicable to claims under contracts of employment.

3 The weekly limit of £158 was applied by The Employment Protection (Variation of Limits) Order 1986 (SI 1986 No 2283) and may be varied in future by Statutory Instrument.

4 In practice, the receiver will act as agent for the Secretary of State in dealing with claims and making payments to the employees (see paragraph 4.29 in the main text).

Payable to Trustees of Occupational Pension Schemes

If there are arrears of either employees' or employers' contributions to an occupational pension scheme at the date of the receiver's appointment (or the date of liquidation, if earlier), the Secretary of State will pay to the trustees or other persons authorised to act on the fund's behalf:

(a) a sum equivalent to the contributions deducted from employees' pay during the twelve months preceding the relevant date but not paid to the fund (EPCA 78 Section 123(5)), plus
(b) the least of:
   (i) the employer's contributions payable but unpaid in respect of the twelve months preceding the relevant date;
  (ii) 10% of the remuneration paid or payable to the employees concerned in respect of the twelve months preceding the relevant date;
 (iii) the amount certified by an actuary as necessary for the scheme to meet its liability for benefits to employees on dissolution (EPCA 78 Section 123(3)).

Reference should be made to the Department of Employment's booklet 'Insolvency of Employers – Safeguard of occupational pension scheme contributions'.

Payable to the Receiver

It is the Secretary of State's practice to pay the receiver a fee for acting as his agent in handling employees' claims, as follows:

Number of employees	*Fee per employee*		
	Basic rate	Receivers' additional premium	Protective award
1–50	£11.80	£8.20	£6.50
51–100	£ 8.30	£6.05	£4.55
101–1,000	£ 5.95	£4.85	£3.40
Over 1,000	£ 4.30	£3.95	£2.85

The receiver's additional premium is payable only to receivers in respect of employees for whom payment in lieu of notice claims are processed in addition to preferential claims.

The above rates apply from 1 April 1987 but are subject to confirmation by the Department of Employment and are reviewed each year.

Appendix G

Reservation of Title Claim Questionnaire

.... IN LIQUIDATION/RECEIVERSHIP

In order to admit any reservation of title claim, it is imperative that the undermentioned questions be answered as fully as possible. Your assistance in this matter would be appreciated.

Name of Supplier: Name of Solicitor:

Address: Address:

Telephone No: Telephone No:
Name of Contract: Name of Contract:

Date ....

1 State the name and quantity of goods which are the subject of your claim to reservation of title.

2 Please supply copies of:

   (a)   the order(s);
   (b)   acknowledgement of order;
   (c)   your delivery note;
   (d)   your invoice(s).

3 If the order was not made in writing, please give details of how the order was placed, the date, and by whom, and the date of the delivery of the goods. Deal with each item separately.

4 Does your firm have a set of standard terms and conditions of sale? If so, please supply a copy and identify the clause which reserved title to the goods to yourselves.

5 (a)   Was a copy of your standard terms and conditions of sale given to the company? If so, when and to whom?
   (b)   What written evidence do you have of acceptance of your terms and conditions by the company?

6 Please provide:

   (a)   A copy of any inventory taken by your representative at the company's premises and the location of the goods at the time.
   (b)   Precise details of the means by which the goods were identified as belonging to the firm and conclusive proof that they were not supplied by any other supplier.

(c) Confirmation as to whether there are any other goods on the premises which have been supplied by yourselves and for which payment has not been made in full or in part.

7 State the amounts of all payments (if any) received from the company in respect of the goods to which you claim reservation of title and provide a copy of your sales ledger account detailing the trading history of the account for the past twelve months.

When completed please return to:

Appendix H.1

Licensing of Insolvency Practitioners

Insolvency
Practitioner
No.

NAME OF PRACTITIONER:

PRINCIPAL BUSINESS ADDRESS:

AUTHORISING BODY (INCLUDING
COMPETENT AUTHORITY):

1 NAME OF PERSON IN RELATION TO
  WHOM THE PRACTITIONER IS ACTING

2 NATURE OF INSOLVENCY PROCEEDING

3 PROGRESS OF ADMINISTRATION
  (entries should be made in respect of all matters applicable to the particular case)

    (i) Date of commencement of insolvency proceeding
    (ii) Date of appointment as insolvency practitioner in insolvency proceeding
    (iii) Date of appointment notified to
        (a)   Registrar of Companies
        (b)   Accountant in Bankruptcy
    (iv) (a)   Date of issue of certificate of specific cover under security requirements
        (b)   Amount of specific cover (£)
        (c)   Name of surety/cautioner
        (d)   Date certificate of cover filed/delivered
    (v) (a)   Date of increase in amount of specific cover
        (b)   Revised amount (£) of cover
        (c)   Date further certificate of cover filed/delivered
    (vi) Date surety/cautioner notified of termination of office
    (vii) (a)   Date of meeting of members
        (b)   Date of first meeting of creditors or of statutory meeting in sequestration
            (i)   to consider an administrator's proposals
            (ii) to consider an administrative receiver's report

    (iii)   in liquidation or bankruptcy
    (iv)   to consider a voluntary arrangement proposal
    (v)   in sequestration or of creditors according to a trust deed for creditors

(viii) Date(s) and purpose of any subsequent meeting(s)

. . . . (1)

. . . . (2)

. . . . (3)

(ix) Disqualification of directors – performance of practitioner's duty under section 7 of the Company Directors' Disqualification Act 1986 to report the conduct of directors

    (a)   Date conduct report submitted to Secretary of State
    (b)   (i)   Date return due
           (ii)   Date return submitted to Secretary of State
    (c)   Date further report(s) submitted, if any

(x) Date of vacation of office

(xi) Date of release or discharge (including date of certificate granted by the Accountant in Bankruptcy)

(xii) Final notice to, or meeting of, creditors

4 DISTRIBUTION TO CREDITORS AND OTHERS

   (i)   For each payment to preferential/preferred creditors

      – Date

      – Amount (p in £)

   (ii)   For each payment to unsecured creditors

      – Date

      – Amount (p in £)

   (iii)   For each return of capital

      – Date

5 FILING OF STATUTORY RETURNS AND ACCOUNTS
(Secretary of State, Registrar of Companies, Accountant in Bankruptcy)

   (i)   In respect of each interim return/abstract of receipts and payments

      Date due

      Date filed

   (ii)   Final return/abstract of accounts

      Date due

      Date filed

Appendix H.2

Notice requiring
Submission of
Administrative
Receivership
Statement of Affairs
No. 3.1 (Rule 3.3)

No.　　　　**of 19**　　.

IN THE HIGH COURT OF JUSTICE

Chancery Division

Companies Court

IN THE MATTER of

AND

IN THE MATTER of The Insolvency Act 1986

(1) Insert full name of administrative receiver.

(2) Insert Full name of person required to submit statement.

Take notice that I (¹)

require you (²)
to submit a Statement as to the Affairs of the Company within　　　　　days.

The Statement must be in the prescribed form and must show:

(i)　particulars of the Company's assets, debts and liabilities
(ii)　the names and addresses of its Creditors
(iii)　the securities held by them respectively
(iv)　the dates when the securities were respectively given

(3) Insert details of further information if required.

(³)

Dated the　　　　　　　19　　.

Signed

Warning
If without reasonable excuse you fail to comply, you will be liable:
(i) On summary conviction to a fine not exceeding the statutory maximum and, for continued contravention, to a daily default fine not exceeding one-tenth of the statutory maximum.
(ii) On conviction on indictment to a fine.

oyez The Solicitors' Law Stationery Society plc, 24 Gray's Inn Road, London WC1X 8HR　　1986 Edition　12.86　BM

5090963

Insolvency-Company 3.1

* * * * *

Statement of Affairs

Statement as to affairs of

_____

On the _____ 19__ the date of the Administrative Receiver's Appointment

Affidavit

This affidavit must be sworn or affirmed before a Solicitor or Commissioner of Oaths when you have completed the rest of this form.

I _____

of _____

_____

Swear/affirm that the several pages attached marked _____ are to the best of my knowledge and belief a full, true and complete statement as the affairs of the above named company as at _____ the date of the appointment of the administrative receiver and that the said company carried on business as

_____

_____

_____

_____

Sworn/affirmed at _____

Date _____

_____

Signatures _____

Before me _____

_____

A Solicitor or Commissioner of Oaths

The Solicitor or Commissioner is particularly requested, before swearing/ affirming the affidavit, to make sure that the full name, address and description of the Deponent are stated, and to initial any crossings-out or other alterations in the printed form. A deficiency in the affidavit in any of the above respects will mean that it is refused by the court, and will necessitate its being re-sworn/re-affirmed.

© January 1987 Fourmat Publishing 27 & 28 St Albans Place Islington Green London N1 ONX

A—Summary of Assets

Assets	Book Value £	Estimated to Realise £
Assets specifically pledged:—		
Assets not specifically pledged:—		
Estimated total assets available for preferential creditors £		

Signature _____   Date _____

A 1–Summary of Liabilities

		Estimated to realise £
Estimated total assets available for preferential creditors (carried from page A)	£	
Liabilities		
Preferential creditors:—	£	
Estimated deficiency/surplus as regards preferential creditors	£	
Debts secured by a floating charge:—	£	
Estimated deficiency/surplus of assets available for non-preferential creditors	£	
Non-preferential claims:—	£	
Estimated deficiency/surplus as regards creditors	£	
Issued and called up capital:—	£	
Estimated total deficiency/surplus as regards members	£	

Signature _____   Date _____

B
Company Creditors

Note You must identify creditors under hire-purchase, chattel leasing or conditional sale agreements *and* customers claiming amounts paid in advance of the supply of goods or services *and* creditors claiming retention of title over property in the company's possession.

Name of creditor or claimant	Address (with postcode)	Amount of debt £	Details of any security held by creditor	Date security given	Value of security £

Signature _____   Date _____

Rule 3.8   **Form 3.3**

The Insolvency Act 1986
Statement of Affairs in **R.3.8(4)**
Administrative Receivership
Following Report to Creditors
Pursuant to Rule 3.8(4) of the
Insolvency Rules 1986

To the Registrar of Companies   **For official use**

Company Number

Name of Company

Insert full name of
company

Limited

I/We _____

of   _____

_____

_____

administrative receiver(s) of the company attach a copy of the statement of affairs
of the company.

Signed _____ Dated _____

Presenter's name,
address and reference
(if any):

For Official Use
Insolvency Section   Post Room

The Insolvency Act 1986
Certificate of Constitution
[Amended Certificate] of   # R.3.17(4)
Creditors' Committee
Pursuant to Rule 3.17(4) of the
Insolvency Rules 1986

To the Registrar of Companies   **For official use**

Company Number

Name of Company

(a) Insert full name of   (a)
company

                                                                       Limited

(b) Insert full name(s)   I/We (b)
and address(es)

administrative receiver(s) of the above company certify that the creditors'
(c) Insert names and   committee has been duly constituted and that the membership is as follows (c)
addresses of members
of committee

d) Delete as necessary   (d) This certificate amends the certificate issued by me on (e)
(e) Insert date of
previous certificate

Signed   Date

Presenter's name,
address and reference
(if any)
                                           For Official Use
                                   Insolvency Section   Post Room

oyez   The Solicitors' Law Stationery Society plc, 24 Gray's Inn Road, London WC1X 8HR   1986 Edition 12.86 BM

5090997

Insolvency-Company 3.4   * * * * *

Rule 3.17

Form 3.5

The Insolvency Act 1986
Administrative Receiver's Report
as to Change in Membership of
Creditors' Committee

R.3.17(5)

Pursuant to Rule 3.17(5) of the
Insolvency Rules 1986

To the Registrar of Companies

For official use

Company Number

Name of Company

(a) Insert full name of company

(a)

Limited

(b) Insert full name(s) and address(es)

I/We (b)

(c) Insert date

administrative receiver(s) of the above company report that the membership of the creditors' committee has altered since the last certificate dated (c)

(d) Insert details of changes in membership

as follows (d)

Signed

Date

Presenter's name, address and reference (if any)

For Official Use
Insolvency Section   Post Room

5091008

Insolvency-Company 3.5   * * * * *

Appendix H.7

M

Form 3.6

Rule 3.32 **The Insolvency Act 1986**

Receiver or Manager or Administrative Receiver's Abstract of Receipts and Payments
Pursuant to section 38 of the Insolvency Act 1986
Rule 3.32(1) of the Insolvency Rules 1986

S.38/R

To the Registrar of Companies

For official use

*Administrative Receivership only

*To the company

*To the members of the creditors' committee

*To the appointor of administrative receiver

Company Number

Name of Company

Insert full name of company

Limited

I/We _____

of _____

_____

_____

Delete as appropriate — appointed [receiver] [manager] [receiver and manager] [administrative receiver] of the company on

Insert date

present overleaf [my] [our]* abstract of receipts and payments for the period from

to

Number of continuation sheets (if any attached)

Signed _____ Date _____

Presenter's name, address and reference (if any)

_____

_____

_____

_____

For Official Use
Insolvency Section   **Post Room**

Abstract

Note
The receipts and
payments must
severally be added up
at the foot of each
sheet and the totals
carried forward from
one abstract to
another without any
intermediate balance
so that the gross
totals shall represent
the total amounts
received and paid by
the receiver since he
was appointed

Receipts	£	p
Brought forward from previous Abstract (if any)	£	p
Carried forward to [continuation sheet]*[next Abstract]		

*delete as appropriate

Payments	£	p
Brought forward from previous Abstract (if any)	£	p
Carried forward to [continuation sheet]*[next Abstract]		

*delete as appropriate

oyez The Solicitors' Law Stationery Society plc, 24 Gray's Inn Road, London WC1X 8HR   1986 Edition 12.86 F6744
5091016
Insolvency—Company 3.6   ★ ★ ★ ★ ★

Form 3.7

The Insolvency Act 1986

Notice of Administrative Receiver's Death

Pursuant to Rule 3.34 of the Insolvency Rules 1986

R.3.34

To the Registrar of Companies

For official use

Company Number

Name of Company

Insert full name of company

Limited

Mr _____

of _____

administrative receiver of the above company died on:

Signed _____ Dated _____

For and on behalf of appointor

Presenter's name, address and reference (if any):

For Official Use

Insolvency Section　　　**Post Room**

oyez The Solicitors' Law Stationery Society plc, 24 Gray's Inn Road, London WC1X 8HR　　1986 Edition 12.86　F6752

5091024

★★★★★

Insolvency—Company 3.7

Appendix H.9

Form 3.8

The Insolvency Act 1986
Notice of Order to Dispose **S.43(5)**
of Charged Property
**Pursuant to section 43(5) of the
Insolvency Act 1986**

To the Registrar of Companies

For official use

Company Number

Name of Company

Insert full name of
company

Limited

I/We _____

of _____

_____

_____

administrative receiver(s) of the company obtained an order under section 43(1) of
the Insolvency Act 1986 to dispose of property which is subject to a security on

An office copy of the said court order is attached

Signed _____ Date _____

Presenter's name,
address and reference
(if any):

For Official Use
Insolvency Section **Post Room**

oyez The Solicitors' Law Stationery Society plc, 24 Gray's Inn Road, London WC1X 8HR   1986 Edition 12.86 F6753

5091032

Insolvency—Company 3.8   ★ ★ ★ ★ ★

Appendix H.10

Notice of Resignation
of Administrative
Receiver Pursuant to
Section 45(1) of The
Insolvency Act 1986.
(Section 45(1)) No. 3.9

IN THE HIGH COURT OF JUSTICE

Chancery Division

Companies Court

IN THE MATTER of

AND

IN THE MATTER of The Insolvency Act 1986

(1) Insert full name
and address of
Administrative
Receiver.

I, (^{1})

(2) Insert date to be at
least 7 days ahead.

the Administrative Receiver of the above Company give notice that I am resigning
from the said office of Administrative Receiver with effect from (^{2})

Signed

Dated the   19   .

(3) Person who made
the Appointment.

To: (^{3})

(4) Company or, if in
Liquidation, the
Liquidator.

(^{4})

oyez   The Solicitors' Law Stationery Society plc, 24 Gray's Inn Road, London WC1X 8HR   1986 Edition 12.86 BM

5091040

Insolvency-Company 3.9   ★ ★ ★ ★ ★

Appendix H.11

Form 3.10

The Insolvency Act 1986
Administrative Receiver's Report

S.48(1)

Pursuant to section 48(1) of the Insolvency
Act 1986 and Rule 3.8(3) of the Insolvency
Rules 1986

To the Registrar of Companies

For official use

```
┌───┬───┬───┐
│   │   │   │
└───┴───┴───┘
```

Company Number

```
┌─────────────────────────┐
│                         │
└─────────────────────────┘
```

Name of Company

Insert full name of
company

```
┌────────────────────────────────────────────────┐
│                                                  │
│                                                  │
│                                        Limited   │
└────────────────────────────────────────────────┘
```

I/We _____

of _____

_____

_____

administrative receiver(s) of the company attach a copy of my [our] report to
creditors and a copy of the statement of affairs of the company

Signed _____ Dated _____

Presenter's name,
address and reference
(if any):

_____

_____

_____

_____

```
┌──────────────────────────────────────┐
│            For Official Use            │
│  Insolvency Section    Post Room       │
│                    │                   │
│                    │                   │
│                    │                   │
└──────────────────────────────────────┘
```

oyez The Solicitors' Law Stationery Society plc, 24 Gray's Inn Road, London WC1X 8HR   1986 Edition 12.86 BM

5091058

Insolvency-Company 3.10   * * * * *

Appendix H.12

Form 8.3: Proxy (Administrative Receivership)

Insolvency Act 1986
Proxy (Administrative Receivership)

In the matter of

Notes to help completion of the form

and in the matter of the Insolvency Act 1986

Please give full name & address for communication

Name of creditor _____

Address _____

_____

Please insert name of person (who must be 18 or over) or the "Chairman of the meeting". If you wish to provide for alternative proxy-holders in the circumstances that your first choice is unable to attend please state the name(s) of the alternatives as well.

Name of proxy-holder _____

_____

_____

_____

_____

_____

_____

_____

_____

_____

_____

Please delete words in brackets if the proxy-holder is only to vote as directed, ie he has no discretion

I appoint the above person to be my/the creditor's proxy-holder at the meeting of creditors to be held on _____,
or at any adjournment of that meeting. The proxy-holder is to propose or vote as instructed below [and in respect of any resolution for which no specific instruction is given, may vote or abstain at his/her discretion].

Voting instructions for resolutions

For the appointment of _____

of _____

_____

representing _____
as a member of the creditors' committee.

This form must be signed

Signature _____   Date _____

Name in CAPITAL LETTERS _____

Only to be completed if the creditor has not signed in person

Position with creditor or relationship to creditor or other authority for signature _____

_____

Remember: there may be resolutions on the other side of this form.

© January 1987   Fourmat Publishing 27 & 28 St Albans Place Islington Green London N1 0NX

Appendix H.13

Notice of appointment of receiver or manager

Pursuant to section 405(1) of the Companies Act 1985

Please do not
write in this
binding margin

**Please complete
legibly, preferably
in black type, or
bold block lettering**

To the Registrar of Companies

For official use

Company number

Name of company

* insert full name
of company

*

I/We _____

of _____

_____

give notice that

ø insert name and
address of
receiver/manager

ø

was appointed as [receiver][manager][receiver and manager]† of [part of] the property of the company.

The appointment was made by

† delete as
appropriate

§ name of court
making the order

[an order of the § _____

_____

made on _____]†

‡ enter description
and date of the
instrument under
which appointment
is made, and state
whether it is a
debenture secured
by a floating charge

[me/us on _____ under the powers contained in‡ _____

_____

_____

_____]†

Signed

Date

Presentor's name address and
reference (if any):

For official Use

Liquidation Section

Post room

Form F260 (No. 405(1))
© Fourmat Publishing
27 & 28 St Albans Place
London N1 0NX

July 1985

Time critical reference

Appendix H.14

COMPANIES FORM No. 405(2)

Notice of ceasing to act as receiver or manager

Pursuant to section 405(2) of the Companies Act 1985

Please do not
write in
this margin

To the Registrar of Companies

For official use

Company number

**Please complete
legibly, preferably
in black type, or
bold block lettering**

Name of company

* insert full name
of company

* _____

I/We _____

_____

of _____

_____

Postcode: _____

† delete as
appropriate

give notice that I/we ceased to act as [receiver][manager][receiver and manager]†

of the above company on _____ 19 _____

Signed

Date

_____

Presentor's name address and
reference (if any):

For official Use

Liquidation Section

Post room

Form F275 (No. 405(2))
© Fourmat Publishing
27 & 28 St Albans Place
London N1 0NX

July 1985

EMPLOYMENT PROTECTION ACT 1975

EMPLOYER'S NOTIFICATION OF PROPOSED REDUNDANCIES UNDER SECTION 100

READ THESE NOTES CAREFULLY BEFORE COMPLETING THE FORM AND SIGNING THE DECLARATION

GENERAL

1 The Employment Protection Act requires employers to notify the Secretary of State for Employment of proposed redundancies involving ten or more dismissals a specified number of days before the first dismissal is to take effect. (See the leaflet Procedure for Handling Redundancies, PL624). Compliance with this requirement does not preclude the employer from postponing or abandoning implementation of the proposals to dismiss if, for example, there is a relevant change of circumstances.

2 Please complete a separate form HRI in respect of each establishment at which 10 or more employees are likely to be dismissed as redundant.

3 This form is designed to cover the information required by the Secretary of State under Part IV of the Employment Protection Act; alternatively you may write a letter which contains the same particulars as in the form. Whichever method you choose, please return the notification using the addressed envelope provided — or, if you did not receive one, send or deliver it to the nearest office of the Department of Employment.

4 A copy of this notification must be sent to representatives of independent trade unions recognised for any of the categories of workers whom it is proposed to dismiss as redundant.

NOTES ON QUESTIONS

Please write the answers in the spaces provided. If appropriate write NIL. If space is insufficient, continue on separate sheet of paper marking the question number and making a note to that effect on this form.

NOTES ON DECLARATION

The declaration should be signed and dated by the employer, or on his behalf by a person of appropriate status. The position held by the signatory should be indicated.

NB

If rebate against redundancy payments is being claimed you should apply to the Department of Employment separately on form RP I which can be obtained from any Redundancy Payments Office, the address of which is available at any Unemployment Benefit Office or Employment Office

---

DEPARTMENT OF EMPLOYMENT

Dd. 8257627 100m 3/81 UPS B/B

HR I

QUESTIONS

1 Name, address and telephone number of employer.

....

....

....

2 Name of person to be contacted in connection with this form (include address and telephone number, if different from Q1).

....

....

....

3 Address of establishment at which employees are employed, (if different from Q1).

....

....

4 Please state the nature of the main business at the establishment named above.

....

5 (a) What are the main reasons for the proposed redundancies at the above named establishment?

(Please tick the appropriate box(es))

Reduced demand for products or services	A
Completion of contract or part of contract	B
Transfer of activities to another establishment following a merger	C
Transfer of activities to another establishment for other reasons	D
Introduction of new plant or machinery	E
Changes in methods or organisation of work	F
Introduction of microelectronics	G
Other reasons	H

(b) If you have ticked boxes D, F or H. please give brief details

....

....

6 (a) What is the total number currently employed at the establishment?

....

(b) What is the total number you anticipate at present MAY be dismissed as redundant at the establishment?

....

(c) If available please give a breakdown of (a) and (b) by occupational groups.

	Employed	Redundant
Manual Skilled		
Semi-skilled		
Unskilled		
Clerical		
Managerial/Technical		

(d) Please state the number of apprentices and long term trainees who may become redundant, if known

....

(e) Please state the number of employees under 20 years old (including apprentices etc) who may become redundant, (if known)

....

(f) Do you propose to close the establishment at which these redundancies may occur?

....

7 On what dates will:

(a) the first proposed redundancy take effect?

Day	Month	Year

(b) the last proposed redundancy take effect?

Day	Month	Year

8 How do you propose to select employees who may be dismissed as redundant? Please give brief details.

....

....

9 Give name(s) and address(es) of trade union(s) recognised for categories of employees it is proposed to dismiss as redundant.

....

....

....

....

....

10 (a) Give date when consultations began with union(s)

Day	Month	Year

(b) Has full agreement been reached?

....

(c) Is the redundancy being handled in accordance with a collective agreement on redundancies?

....

If you answer YES please give brief details or send a copy of the agreement.

....

DECLARATION

I certify that the information given on this form is correct to the best of my knowledge.

Signature ....

Position held ....

Date ....

FOR DEPARTMENTAL USE		
1	2	3
4	5	6
7	8	

Appendix H.16

Report on Conduct of Directors by an
Administrative Receiver
under Section 7(3) of the Company Directors Disqualification Act, 1986

D2

**Before completing this form
read the DTI Guidance Notes**

		Official Use
Company registered number		
Name of Company		
Registered Office address		
Nature of Business		
Trading Names		
Principal place of business		
Date of appointment of Administrative Receiver		
Name of Administrative Receiver		
Office holder number		
Administrative Receiver's address		
Period covered by report	From: To:	

1. I am the administrative receiver of the company and it appears to me that the persons listed in the schedule were either directors or shadow directors of the company and **were the only** such directors of the company during the period covered by this report.

2. It further appears to me that the conduct of each of the persons in respect of whom I have marked Y in column 5 in the schedule as a director of the company, either considered in relation to this company alone or taken together with his conduct as a director of any other company, makes him unfit to be concerned in the management of a company. Details of his conduct are provided in Part D2(B) of the report.

Schedule

1 Full name and other known names	2 Last known address	3 Mark X if shadow Director	4 Period as Director From To	5 If you have attached supplementary details please mark with a Y

Administrative Receiver's Signature _____

Date _____

Remember to attach forms D2(A) and D2(B)

Appendix H.17

Part A

Further Details of the Company

D2(A)

Name of Company

3	Date of incorporation		
4	Period of trading	From _____	To _____
5	Estimated assets available for		

● preferential creditors:

● unsecured creditors:

6 Summary of statement of affairs   £

Gross assets: _____

Gross liabilities to creditors: _____

Estimated total deficiency as regards creditors: _____

Called-up capital: _____

7 Approximate number and value of unsecured creditors distinguishing between   No.   £

Trade and expense: _____   _____

Depositor or consumer pre-paid: _____   _____

Connected companies: _____   _____

Other: _____   _____

---

8   Details of connected companies with which the company has had any dealings

The above is correct to the best of my knowledge, information and belief

Administrative Receiver's Signature _____

Date _____

Appendix H.18

A separate "Part B" is to be completed for each
Director to be reported upon.

Part B

Name of Company

Fuller Details of the Individual Director
Subject to this Report

---

9   Full name of the Director:

10   Date of birth:

11   Occupation, trade or profession;

12 Position(s) held within company:

---

13   Give details (on such additional pages as necessary) of the conduct of the director, which makes it appear to
     you that the conditions of Section 6(1) are satisfied. You should have particular regard to Schedule 1 of
     the Act.

14   List the remuneration and other benefits during each of the 3 years to the relevant date in relation to the
     company as defined in Rule 4.1.

Period ended	Remuneration received	Remuneration voted	Cash expenses	Benefits in kind
	£	£	£	£
_____	_____	_____	_____	_____
_____	_____	_____	_____	_____
_____	_____	_____	_____	_____
_____	_____	_____	_____	_____

15(a)   Other companies of which the director is or was during the 3 years to the relevant date in relation to the company as defined under Rule 4.1 also a director or shadow director.

Name of Company	Reg. No.	Are you also the Liquidator, Administrative Receiver or Administrator of that Company (Y/N)	Mark X here if you are to submit a conduct report in respect of the Company or enter date of report if already submitted

15(b)   Give details of any other companies not listed at Q8 or 15(a) above with which the director may have had an association which you feel may be relevant to the consideration of his conduct.

16   Give brief details of any civil or criminal proceedings in relation to the company taken or likely to be taken against the director.

17   Are there any other matter(s) which you consider the Secretary of State should take into consideration.

The details given in Part D2(B) (comprising _____ pages)
are correct to the best of my knowledge, information and belief.

Administrative Receiver's Signature _____

Date _____

On completion please return to: **Department of Trade and Industry**
                                             Disqualification Unit
                                             6th Floor
                                             Companies House
                                             55-71 City Road
                                             London EC1Y 1BB

Return of Directors by an
Administrative Receiver under
Rule 4 of the Insolvent Companies
(Report on Conduct of Directors) No. 2 Rules 1986

D5

**Before completing this form
read the DTI Guidance Notes**

		Official Use
Company registered number		
Name of Company		
Registered Office address		
Nature of Business		
Trading Names		
Principal place of business		
Date of appointment of Administrative Receiver		
Name of Administrative Receiver		
Office holder number		
Administrative Receiver's address		

1 (i) I have not submitted a report in this case because

Mark with
an X the
statement
which applies

a ☐ as at the date of this return I have not become aware of any matters which would require me to make a report under Section 7(3) of the Act

b ☐ sufficient information is not yet to hand (see below).

(ii) I have not submitted a report on all of the directors in this case because:

c ☐ as at the date of this return I have not become aware of any matters which would require me to make a report under Section 7(3) of the Act on the remaining directors

d ☐ sufficient information is not yet to hand (see below)

If you have marked box b or box d please indicate the likely date when the report if any will be submitted: _____   _____

Month   Year

2 The persons listed in the schedule were to the best of my knowledge and belief **all** the persons who were directors or shadow directors of the company during the three years prior to the relevant date in relation to the company as determined under rule 4(4)(c).

Schedule

Full name and other known names	Last known address	Mark X if shadow Director	Period as Director From To

On completion please return to:
**Department of Trade and Industry
Disqualification Unit
6th Floor, Companies House
55-71 City Road
London EC1Y 1BB**

Administrative Receiver's Signature _____

Date _____

Appendix I.1

Confirmation of Acceptance of Appointment as Administrative Receiver(s)

To:

Name of company:

I/We,

of

acknowledge receipt of the instrument appointing me/us administrative receiver(s) of

which was received by me/us or on my/our behalf at   am/pm

on

I am/We are pleased to confirm that such appointment was accepted by me/us at   on

Signed: Date:

. . . .

NOTES

1   This confirmation must be delivered to the appointor within seven days of receiving the instrument of appointment.

2   In the case of a joint appointment, if both or all appointees accepted the appointment at the same time this form should be signed by them all. If the appointment was accepted at different times, a separate form should be completed by each appointee but if possible they should be delivered to the appointor simultaneously.

3   The confirmation may be signed on an appointee's behalf by anyone he authorises to do so. His representative should sign his own name and add beneath his signature 'Duly authorised to sign on behalf of . . . . '.

Appendix I.2

Notice to Company of Appointment of Administrative Receiver Pursuant to Section 46(1)(A) of the Insolvency Act 1986

Company number

To:

Name of company:

I/We,

of

hereby give notice that on the .... day of .... 19....
I was/we were appointed administrative receiver(s) of the above named company
by .... Bank Plc under the terms of a debenture dated .... giving
the holders a fixed and floating charge over (the whole) (substantially the whole) of
the assets of the company.

....

Notes:

Trading name if different from above:

Other name(s) by which the company was
called in the twelve months preceding the
appointment:

Other trading names used by the company
in that period:

Description of assets (if any) not covered
by the appointment:

Appendix I.3

To All Creditors

Notice of Appointment of Administrative Receiver Pursuant to Section 46(1)(B) of the Insolvency Act 1986

Company number

Name of company:

I/We,

of

hereby give notice that on the .... day of .... 19....
I was/we were appointed administrative receiver(s) of the above named company
by .... Bank Plc under the terms of a debenture dated .... giving
the holders a fixed and floating charge over (the whole) (substantially the whole) of
the assets of the company.

. . . .

Notes:

Trading name if different from above:

Other name(s) by which the company was
called in the twelve months preceding the
appointment:

Other trading names used by the company
in that period:

Description of assets (if any) not covered
by the appointment:

Appendix I.4

Notice of Appointment of Joint Administrative Receivers

We,   of

were appointed joint administrative receivers of

Registered number

by   on

. . . .

NOTES: (Delete if inapplicable)

Trading name if different from that stated above:

Other name(s) by which the company was called in the twelve months preceding the appointment:

Other trading names used by the company in that period:

Appendix I.5

Advertisement of Creditors' Meeting Under Section 48(2) of the Insolvency Act 1986

Registered No   Registered in

LIMITED

NOTICE IS HEREBY GIVEN, pursuant to section 48(2) of the Insolvency Act 1986, that a meeting of the unsecured creditors of the above named company will be held at

at   hours on

for the purpose of having laid before it a copy of the report prepared by the administrative receiver(s) under section 48 of the said Act. The meeting may, if it thinks fit, establish a committee to exercise the functions conferred on creditors' committees by or under the Act.

Creditors are only entitled to vote if:

(a) they have delivered to me/us at the address shown below, no later than 1200 hours on   , written details of the debts they claim to be due to them from the company, and the claim has been duly admitted under the provisions of Rule 3.11 of the Insolvency Rules 1986; and

(b) there has been lodged with me/us any proxy which the creditor intends to be used on his behalf.

Signed: Date:

Administrative receiver(s)

. . . .

NOTE (Delete if inapplicable)

Creditors may obtain a copy of the report, free of charge, on application to the administrative receiver(s) at the address shown above.

. . . .

Name(s) of signatory(ies) in block capitals:

(for information of printer)

Appendix I.6

Notice of Creditors' Meeting Under Section 48(2) of the Insolvency Act 1986

Registered No   Registered in

LIMITED

NOTICE IS HEREBY GIVEN, pursuant to section 48(2) of the Insolvency Act 1986, that a meeting of the unsecured creditors of the above named company will be held at

at   hours on

for the purpose of having laid before it a copy of the report prepared by the administrative receiver(s) under section 48 of the said Act. The meeting may, if it thinks fit, establish a committee to exercise the functions conferred on creditors' committees by or under the Act.

A proxy form is sent herewith. Creditors whose claims are wholly secured are not entitled to attend or be represented at the meeting. Other creditors are only entitled to vote if:

(a)   they have delivered to me/us at the address shown below, no later than 1200 hours on   , written details of the debts they claim to be due to them from the company, and the claim has been duly admitted under the provisions of Rule 3.11 of the Insolvency Rules 1986; and

(b)   there has been lodged with me/us any proxy which the creditor intends to be used on his behalf.

Signed: Date:

Administrative receiver(s)

. . . .

NOTE (Delete whichever is inapplicable)

A copy of the report is being sent to creditors herewith/separately.

Creditors may obtain a copy of the report, free of charge, on application to the administrative receiver(s) at the address shown above.

Appendix I.7

Notice of Availability of Administrative Receiver's Report

TO THE CREDITORS OF:

I/We,

of

the administrative receiver(s) of the above named company, HEREBY GIVE NOTICE that creditors of the company may obtain, free of charge, copies of the report I/we have prepared under section 48 of the Insolvency Act 1986 by applying to me/us in writing at the above address (quoting reference   ).

SIGNED:

DATE:

....

NOTE:

      I/We have applied to the court for an order under section 48(2) of the said Act dispensing with the requirement that a meeting of the company's creditors be held. Such application is to be heard at

      on   at

....

The above note should, of course, be deleted if no such application has been made.

Appendix I.8

Certificate of Insolvency for the Purposes of Section 22(3)(b) of the Value Added Tax Act 1983

Company:

Registered in England
Registered No.

Date:

I,

of

having been appointed joint administrative receiver of

on

hereby certify that, in my opinion, if it went into liquidation the assets of the company would be insufficient to cover the payment of any dividend in respect of debts which are neither preferential nor secured.

. . . .

Appendix J.1

Specimen letter to directors and secretary

RECORDED DELIVERY

The Directors and Secretary

Dear Sirs,

          LIMITED IN RECEIVERSHIP

I am writing to inform you that on   my partner,   , and I were appointed joint administrative receivers of the above named company by   Bank Plc under the terms of a debenture dated   giving the holders a fixed and floating charge over the whole of the assets of the company.

I enclose, in duplicate, formal notice of my appointment as joint administrative receiver and should be grateful if you would acknowledge this by signing and returning one copy to me.

In accordance with Section 47 of the Insolvency Act 1986, I require you to prepare and submit to me a detailed statement of affairs of the company in statutory form as provided by such Act, within the course of the next 21 days, for which I enclose the formal notice on Form 3.1. [See appendix H.2].

Should you require professional assistance with the preparation of this statement, please advise me without delay as I am, if necessary, empowered to allow such costs as I consider reasonable to be met out of the assets of the company.

I would also advise you that the effect of my appointment as administrative receiver is to suspend your powers of management but it must be emphasised that your statutory obligations as a director/secretary of the company continue.

I am required by Rule 3.3 of the Insolvency Rules 1986 to inform you of the application to you, and to all others to whom the notice has been sent, of Section 235 of the Insolvency Act 1986. This obliges you to:

(a)   give me such information concerning the company and its promotion, formation, business, dealings, affairs or property as I may reasonably require; and

(b)   attend on me at such times as I may reasonably require.

A list of the names and addresses of all persons to whom this notice has been sent is attached/listed below.*

Yours truly,

Joint administrative receiver

*Delete as appropriate

126

Appendix J.2

Specimen letter to request advertisement of appointment

Dear Sirs,

<u>   LIMITED IN RECEIVERSHIP</u>

Further to my appointment as joint administrative receiver of the above company I enclose the notice of the appointment for advertising once in the London Gazette and once in an appropriate newspaper. [See appendix I.4].

Please submit your invoice in the usual manner.

Yours truly,

Joint administrative receiver

Appendix J.3

Specimen letter to the bank

The Manager

        Bank Plc

Dear Sir,

<u>   LIMITED IN RECEIVERSHIP</u>

Following the acceptance by my partner,   , and I of the appointment as joint administrative receivers of the above company, I enclose the formal notice of confirmation of our acceptance. [See appendix I.1].

I should be grateful if you would confirm that the notice of our appointment has been filed with the Registrar of Companies.

Yours truly,

Joint administrative receiver

128

Appendix J.4

Specimen letter to solicitors to advise on validity

Dear Sir,

<u>LIMITED IN RECEIVERSHIP</u>

I wish to advise you that my partner,   , and I were appointed joint administrative receivers of the above named company by   Bank Plc under the terms of a debenture dated   giving the holders a fixed and floating charge over the whole of the assets of the company.

I am enclosing the following:

(a)   a copy of the charge document and the certificate of registration
(b)   a copy of the company's memorandum and articles of association
(c)   copies of the company and board minutes evidencing the appointment of the signatories, the approval of the charge and the authority for its execution
(d)   details of the events giving rise to the right to appoint an administrative receiver
(e)   details of the amount due from the company to the charge holder
(f)   a copy of the instrument of appointment, and
(g)   a copy of the confirmation of acceptance.

I should be grateful if you would please confirm:

(a)   that the bank's charges are in order
(b)   the extent to which the assets of the company are covered by the fixed and floating charge
(c)   that the appointment of ourselves as joint administrative receivers is in order, and
(d)   the extent of our powers to deal with the assets of the company with details of any limitations thereon.

An early reply to this letter would be appreciated.

Yours truly,

Joint administrative receiver

Appendix J.5

Specimen letter to branch bankers to open receivership account

The Manager
      Bank Plc

Dear Sir,

<u>   LIMITED IN RECEIVERSHIP</u>

I enclose a copy of the deed by which my partner,   , and I were appointed joint administrative receivers of the above company on   under the terms of a debenture dated

Would you please open a new account to be designated: '   joint administrative receivers,   Limited' and forward to me as soon as possible a cheque book containing 50 cheques made payable to order, together with paying-in books. My accounts department will be writing to you with the relevant documentation, but in the meantime all cheques will be signed by either Mr   or myself. A specimen signature form is enclosed.

I would confirm that no cheques presented for payment after the date of my appointment on the company's old accounts or any standing order or direct debit becoming due after that date, should be met unless confirmed by me *in writing*. I should be grateful if you would advise me or my manager on a daily basis of cheques being presented for payment. It would also be helpful if you could send me a schedule of all standing orders or direct debits.

I will be writing under separate cover concerning future banking facilities, but I would confirm that bank statements should be forwarded on a weekly basis to the company's premises and to my office at

In the meantime, would you please provide me with the undermentioned information:

(a) Details of all accounts operated by the company prior to my appointment.
(b) Details of any arrangements with regard to bonding, ECGD facilities or other accounts which should be included under the bank's security.
(c) Details of all leases or title deeds held by the bank as security, with copies of the leases.
(d) Details of any valuations of the company's assets carried out on the bank's behalf and the reasons for such valuations.
(e) Details of any other securities such as share certificates, which may be held to the company's account which may form part of the bank's security and/or the company's assets.
(f) Any other matters which you feel should be brought to my attention.

I look forward to hearing from you as soon as possible and should there be any queries arising, please do not hesitate to contact me.

Yours truly,

Joint administrative receiver

130

Appendix J.6

Specimen letter to banks where no accounts to be maintained

The Manager
      Bank Plc

Dear Sir,

<u>   LIMITED IN RECEIVERSHIP</u>

I enclose a copy of the deed of appointment of my partner,   , and I as joint administrative receivers of the above company on   under the terms of a debenture dated

I confirm that no cheques presented for payment after the date of my appointment on the company's accounts or any standing order or direct debit becoming due after that date should be met unless confirmed by me *in writing*.

I should be grateful if you would advise me or my manager on a daily basis of cheques being presented for payment. It would also be helpful if you would send me a schedule of all standing orders or direct debits.

I should also be grateful if you would forward to the above address a cheque for the balance on the company's account made payable to '   joint administrative receiver,   Limited'.

Would you please also provide me with the following information:

(a) Details of all accounts operated by the company prior to my appointment.
(b) Details of any arrangements with regard to bonding, ECGD facilities or other accounts which should be included under the bank's security.
(c) Details of all leases or title deeds held by the bank as security, with copies of the leases.
(d) Details of any valuations of the company's assets carried out on the bank's behalf and the reasons for such valuations.
(e) Details of any other securities such as share certificates, which may be held to the company's account which may form part of the bank's security and/or the company's assets.
(f) Any other matters which you feel should be brought to my attention.

I look forward to hearing from you as soon as possible and should there be any queries arising, please do not hesitate to contact me.

Yours truly,

Joint administrative receiver

Appendix J.7

Specimen letter to receivers' insurers

Dear Sirs,

<u>   LIMITED IN RECEIVERSHIP</u>

I am writing to inform you that my partner,   , and I were appointed joint administrative receivers of the above company on   by   Bank Plc under the terms of a debenture giving the holders a fixed and floating charge over the whole of the assets of the company.

I should be grateful if you would liaise with the company's insurance brokers,   , and confirm that our open cover insurance is in force.

A completed initial advice form will follow shortly.

I look forward to hearing from you.

Yours truly,

Joint administrative receiver

Appendix J.8

Specimen letter to the valuers

Dear Sirs,

<u>LIMITED IN RECEIVERSHIP</u>

As you are aware, my partner,   , and I were appointed joint administrative receivers of the above company on   by   Bank Plc under the terms of a debenture dated   giving the holders a fixed and floating charge over the whole of the assets of the company.

I am writing to confirm my instructions for you to prepare a valuation, both on a going concern and forced sale basis, of the company's physical assets as soon as possible to include all properties, plant, machinery, motor vehicles, fixtures and fittings and stock and work-in-progress including finished goods.

Would you please provide me with global figures on a verbal basis within a period of seven days together with a written description and report on the properties. I would expect to receive a detailed report on the remaining assets within two weeks from the date of my appointment.

In carrying out your valuations I would ask you to note specifically those items which are subject to hire purchase or lease purchase agreements with an estimate of the equity therein. Items on lease should be scheduled separately with an indication as to whether there is any benefit in such leases being assigned to a prospective purchaser of the business. Obviously, you will exclude from your total valuations the value of these leased items.

I look forward to hearing from you.

Yours truly,

Joint administrative receiver

Appendix J.9

Specimen letter to the surveyors

Dear Sirs,

<u>   LIMITED IN RECEIVERSHIP</u>

As you are aware, my partner,   , and I were appointed joint administrative receivers of the above company on   by   Bank Plc under the terms of a debenture dated   giving the holders a fixed and floating charge over the whole of the assets of the company.

I am writing to confirm my instructions for you to prepare a valuation, both on a going concern and forced sale basis, as at the date of my appointment of the company's contracts in progress, contract debtor balances and retentions contract by contract, having regard to the existence of common contract employers. Would you please provide me with global figures on a verbal basis within a period of three days together with a written report within seven days.

Also, I should be grateful if, following discussions with me or my representatives, you would assist in the assignment or determination of any contracts and negotiations with contract employers.

Yours truly,

Joint administrative receiver

Appendix J.10

Specimen letter to creditors

TO ALL CREDITORS

Dear Sirs,

<u>   LIMITED IN RECEIVERSHIP</u>

Registered Office and
Trading Address:

I would advise you that my partner,   , and I were appointed joint administrative receivers of the above named company on   under the terms of a debenture dated   giving the debenture holders fixed and floating charges over the whole of the assets of the company.

In accordance with the provisions of the Insolvency Act 1986 I enclose a notice of our appointment [see appendix I.3], and I also confirm that the directors have been requested to provide me with a statement of affairs as at the date of my appointment. In the meantime, arrangements have been made for the business to continue pending my investigations.

Please note that payment for goods delivered subsequent to my appointment will only be made where delivery is against an order countersigned by me or my authorised representative, Mr   , a specimen of whose signature is given below.

If you have goods awaiting delivery for which you have an order placed prior to my appointment, you must obtain written confirmation that the goods are still required prior to delivery. It should also be understood that by accepting these goods I am not adopting any long term supply contracts into which the company may have entered prior to my appointment.

It should be noted that goods sold and delivered by the company after my appointment on   must be paid for in full and no lien or right of set-off may be applied against such orders in respect of any claims against the company outstanding at that date.

You will understand that I am not in a position to deal with claims of unsecured creditors but it would be appreciated if you would submit a detailed statement of the amounts owing to you as at the close of business on   to
Limited in Receivership, in order that your claim may be scheduled and passed to the directors for inclusion in their statement of affairs.

If you are of the opinion that your claim should be afforded preference in accordance with Section 40 of the Insolvency Act 1986, a note to this effect should be added.

In addition, if you claim any title to goods delivered to the company or any lien over goods in your possession which are the property of the company, please contact me as soon as possible providing full details and copies of supporting documentation.

I will be preparing a report in connection with the affairs of the company which will be sent to you as soon as practicable. This report will be laid before a meeting of creditors within three months of the date of my appointment, the meeting being convened at not less than 14 days' notice.

Any creditor interested in acquiring the goodwill, assets and undertaking of the company should apply to me for full details as soon as possible. In the meantime, if there is any further information you require please do not hesitate to communicate with me or my representative.

Yours truly,

Joint administrative receiver

Mr   will sign   . . . .

Appendix J.11

Specimen letter to directors and managers of the company

Dear Sirs,

<u>   LIMITED IN RECEIVERSHIP</u>

I would advise you that my partner,   , and I were appointed joint administrative receivers of the above company on   by   Bank Plc under the terms of a debenture giving the holders a fixed and floating charge over the whole of the assets of the company.

It is my intention to operate the company's business for the time being and I would draw to your attention that, while you continue to be employed by the company, you are to act only under my instructions.

In this connection, and until further notice, would you please note the following:

(a)   Without my sanction or that of my manager:
      (i)   No orders are to be placed for the purchase of any goods.
    (ii)   No delivery of goods are to be *accepted* or goods *despatched*.
  (iii)   No goods are to be sent out other than in my name as joint administrative receiver.
  (iv)   No contracts are to be entered into or the company's credit pledged.

(b)   All letters, orders, invoices and other outgoing documentation must be headed up with the names of the joint administrative receivers, the date of appointment and the words 'in receivership' after the company's name.

(c)   All incoming post should be passed to my representative in room   and any writs, walking possession orders or petitions for the winding-up of the company must be referred to me immediately.

(d)   All credit cards, of whatever nature, should be withdrawn as of today's date. Cash floats will be provided when required.

(e)   It should be noted that the company must comply with all Government regulations currently in force, including those in respect of fire, buildings, safety, food and hygiene.

(f)   Under no circumstances should any member of the staff speak to the press or other media. Any enquiries in this respect should be directed to myself or my manager.

Receivership instructions have been issued to the personnel/wages, sales, purchasing, production, accounts and transport departments. Please would you ensure that the relevant instructions have been received and are being implemented by all members of your department.

Yours truly,

Joint administrative receiver

Appendix J.12

Specimen letter to the district secretary of all trade unions recognised by the company

Dear Sir,

<u>   LIMITED IN RECEIVERSHIP</u>

I would advise you that my partner,   , and I were appointed joint administrative receivers of the above company on   by   Bank Plc under the terms of a debenture giving the holders a fixed and floating charge over the whole of the assets of the company. I am also advised that your trade union has been recognised by the company.

It is my intention, for the time being, to continue the company's business. Nevertheless, I anticipate that there will be redundancies among the employees.

Under Section 99 of the Employment Protection Act 1975 and Regulation 10 of The Transfer of Undertakings (Protection of Employment) Regulations 1981, the company, as the employer of employees in respect of which a trade union is recognised, is obliged to consult with that trade union about proposed redundancies and on the implication of a possible transfer of the company's business. A copy of the form HR1 sent to the Department of Employment is enclosed for your attention.

As you are aware, the lack of funds makes it almost inevitable that there will be redundancies but at this stage there is considerable uncertainty as to the number and when they will occur.

In the meantime we are considering a transfer of the business to a subsidiary in order to facilitate its continuance and, hopefully, its eventual sale. In order to comply with Section 99 and Regulation 10, I, as agent of the company, the employer, give you notice of the transfer at short notice and likely redundancies. I will, of course, try to give you as much notice as I can of any impending redundancies and the likely transfer of the business.

Under Regulation 4 of The Transfer of Undertakings (Protection of Employment) Regulations 1981 this will be deemed not to be a relevant transfer for the purpose of those regulations and employees will continue to be employed by the present company unless and until they are made redundant or the subsidiary or business is transferred to a purchaser.

If you wish to discuss any of these matters, I should be grateful if you would arrange for your representative to contact me.

Yours truly,

Joint administrative receiver

138

Appendix J.13

Specimen letter to the Redundancy Payments Section of local DoE office

Dear Sirs,

<u>   LIMITED IN RECEIVERSHIP</u>

I am writing to advise you that on   my partner,   , and I were appointed joint administrative receivers of the above named company under the terms of a debenture dated   . The company trades from premises at

Section 100 of the Employment Protection Act 1975 obliges the company to advise the Department about proposed dismissals on the basis of redundancy and requires that such consultation shall begin at the earliest opportunity. If there are special circumstances compliance with the strict requirements of the Section is dispensed with.

As you will be aware, in any case where an administrative receiver has been appointed, lack of funds makes it almost inevitable that there will be redundancies and you will appreciate that very often it is not possible to forecast the number of employees and which employees are to be made redundant until very shortly before the redundancy has to take effect.

In order, therefore, to comply as far as possible with the employer's duties under the said Acts to give you notice that there are special circumstances which render it not reasonably practicable for the employer in this case to comply with all the requirements of Section 100, I, as agent of the company, the employer, give you notice that there will almost inevitably be redundancies. I will, of course, try to give you as much notice as I can of the actual redundancies but it is likely that I will have to make decisions at very short notice.

Yours truly,

Joint administrative receiver

Appendix J.14

Specimen letter to staff being dismissed immediately following appointment

Dear Sir/Madam,

<u>   LIMITED IN RECEIVERSHIP</u>

My partner,   , and I were appointed joint administrative receivers of the above named company on   by   Bank Plc under the terms of a debenture giving the holders a fixed and floating charge over the whole of the assets of the company.

In my capacity as agent for the company, I regret to advise you that the company is no longer in a position to make payments for services rendered by you under its contract of employment with you. You should therefore regard your service as terminated from today's date.

Under the insolvency provisions of the Employment Protection (Consolidation) Act 1978, any claim you may have for money in lieu of notice will, subject to certain limitations, be paid to you by the Department of Employment out of the Redundancy Fund. *After the statutory minimum notice period* to which you are entitled has expired, please complete and return the form IP2 to the address shown.

You are required to mitigate, as far as possible, any claim for money in lieu of notice. Consequently, you should ensure that you claim any social security benefits to which you may be entitled and make efforts to obtain other employment.

Employees who have completed at least two years' continuous service with the company and who are within the age limits laid down by the Employment Protection (Consolidation) Act 1978 should qualify for redundancy pay. Payment of any amount due to you cannot be made by the company and therefore your form RP21 should be sent to the Department of Employment, Redundancy Payments Office.

Monies have been made available to the company to pay your wages and any accrued holiday pay up to tonight (   ). Your P45, outstanding wages and accrued holiday pay will be sent from the company's wages and salaries office during the course of the next week unless alternative arrangements are made for you to collect them personally.

Yours truly,

Joint administrative receiver

Appendix J.15

Specimen letter to staff being retained

Dear

<u>LIMITED IN RECEIVERSHIP</u>

I am writing to inform you that on   my partner,   , and I were appointed joint administrative receivers of the above company by   Bank Plc under the terms of a debenture dated   giving the holders fixed and floating charges over the whole of the assets of the company.

As the agent of the company I intend, for the time being, to permit the company to continue trading while the situation is assessed.

You will continue to be employed by the company and funds will be made available to enable the company to pay you as previously until further notice. I am not adopting your contract of employment; I am acting solely as the company's agent and you will appreciate that I cannot accept any personal liability in respect of your employment.

I shall be grateful if you will continue to carry out your duties as before. If you have any questions for me or my representative please raise them through the usual channels.

Yours truly,

Joint administrative receiver
acting as agent of the company

Appendix J.16

Specimen letter to staff who are employed under a service contract

Dear Sir,

<u>   LIMITED IN RECEIVERSHIP</u>

As you will be aware, my partner,   , and I were appointed joint administrative receivers of the above company on   by   Bank Plc under the terms of a debenture giving the holders a fixed and floating charge over the whole of the assets of the company.

I understand that you have a service contract of employment with the company which has an unexpired term. Although arrangements have been made to provide the company with funds in order to meet your salary on a weekly basis, I am writing to confirm that as joint administrative receiver I am not adopting your service agreement.

Any claim which may arise under your service agreement will rank as an unsecured claim against the company.

Yours truly,

Joint administrative receiver
acting as agent of the company

Appendix J.17

Specimen letter to the Sheriff

Dear Sir,

<u>LIMITED IN RECEIVERSHIP</u>

I would advise you that my partner,   , and I were appointed joint administrative receivers of the above company on   by   Bank Plc under the terms of a debenture giving the holders a fixed and floating charge over the whole of the assets of the company.

I enclose a copy of the deed by which I was appointed joint administrative receiver and should be grateful if you would confirm by return that you agree that the title of the debenture holder prevails over the execution creditor and that you will release to me the goods over which execution has been levied or, alternatively, the proceeds of sale.

Yours truly,

Joint administrative receiver

Appendix J.18

Specimen letter to creditors or solicitors of creditors who have served writs

Dear Sirs,

<u>_____ LIMITED IN RECEIVERSHIP</u>

I would advise you that my partner, _____ , and I were appointed joint administrative receivers of the above company on _____ by _____ Bank Plc under the terms of a debenture giving the holders a fixed and floating charge over the whole of the assets of the company.

I understand that you have served a writ against the company for recovery of the sum of £ _____ . You will realise that by reason of my appointment you will not be able to enforce any judgment obtained by levying execution, and in order to avoid unnecessary costs you may wish to consider deferring further steps in your action.

Yours truly,

Joint administrative receiver

144

Appendix J.19

Specimen letter to transport companies

Dear Sirs,

<u>LIMITED IN RECEIVERSHIP</u>

I would advise you that my partner,   , and I were appointed joint administrative receivers of the above company on   under the terms of a debenture dated   giving the holders a fixed and floating charge over the whole of the assets of the company.

I should be grateful if you would kindly note that I will not be responsible for the payment of carriage or warehouse charges incurred subsequent to my appointment except against instructions which bear my signature or the signature of my manager, Mr   . A specimen of Mr   's signature is given below.

I intend to continue the company's business for the time being and wish to use your services. However, before so doing I will require confirmation from you that you will not attempt to claim a lien on any goods which come into your possession subsequent to my appointment against charges due to you by the company in respect of services rendered by you prior to my appointment. No instructions will be given to you until you confirm by signing and returning the attached duplicate of this letter.

I look forward to hearing from you.

Yours truly,

Joint administrative receiver

Mr   will sign   ....

Add to duplicate letter:

We,   Limited, hereby confirm that we will not attempt to claim a lien on any goods which come into our possession subsequent to your appointment against charges due to us by the company for services rendered by us prior to your appointment.

.... Director

.... Date

Appendix J.20

Specimen letter to customers who are also creditors of the company

Dear Sirs,

<u>   LIMITED IN RECEIVERSHIP</u>
Registered office and
trading address:

I would advise you that my partner,   , and I were appointed joint administrative receivers of the above company on   under the terms of a debenture dated   giving the holders a fixed and floating charge over the whole of the assets of the company.

I understand that you have an outstanding order with the company and wish to place future orders. However, it does appear that you are owed monies by   Limited and are therefore creditors of that company.

In my capacity as agent for the company I regret to advise you that I am unable to authorise the despatch of any goods to you until such time as I receive your written confirmation that you will make payment in full for such supplies and will not exercise any right of set-off, lien or counter claim in respect of monies owing to you as at the date of my appointment. *(Furthermore, I have found it necessary to alter the terms under which goods will be supplied in future and these are set out in the schedule attached to this letter.)*

I should be grateful if you would confirm your agreement to the arrangements as set out above by signing and returning the duplicate copy of this letter.

Yours truly,

Joint administrative receiver

Add to duplicate:

We,   Limited, confirm our agreement to the terms under which future supplies will be made by   Limited in receivership.

. . . . Director

. . . . Date

Appendix J.21

Specimen letter to solicitors

Dear Sirs,

<u>LIMITED IN RECEIVERSHIP</u>

I would advise you that my partner,   , and I were appointed joint administrative receivers of the above company on   by   Bank Plc under the terms of a debenture giving the holders a fixed and floating charge over the whole of the assets of the company.

I enclose a copy of the deed by which I was appointed joint administrative receiver and should be obliged if you would, as soon as possible, give me a short report on all matters which you are at present handling on behalf of the company. In the meantime, would you please not proceed with any current work until further notice.

Please also advise whether you are holding any documents or securities on the company's behalf.

Yours truly,

Joint administrative receiver

Appendix J.22

Specimen letter to company's auditors

Dear Sirs,

<u>LIMITED IN RECEIVERSHIP</u>

I would advise you that my partner,   , and I were appointed joint administrative receivers of the above company on   by   Bank Plc under the terms of a debenture giving the holders a fixed and floating charge over the whole of the assets of the company. For your information I enclose a copy of the deed by which I was appointed joint administrative receiver.

Would you please advise me of any outstanding matters with which you are dealing on behalf of the company together with a brief résumé of any outstanding taxation matters. Would you also provide me with a schedule of any documents of title or statutory books of account which you are holding in your possession.

I look forward to hearing from you.

Yours truly,

Joint administrative receiver

Appendix J.23

Specimen letter to debtors of the company

Dear Sirs,

<u>   LIMITED IN RECEIVERSHIP</u>

I would advise you that my partner,   , and I were appointed joint administrative receivers of the above company on   by   Bank Plc under the terms of a debenture giving the holders a fixed and floating charge over the whole of the assets of the company.

From my preliminary examination of the company's records it appears that there is a sum of £   due from you (*as detailed in the enclosed statement of account*) and I should therefore be grateful if you would let me have a remittance for that amount within the next fourteen days. Cheques should be made payable to 'the joint administrative receivers   Limited'.

Yours truly,

Joint administrative receiver

Appendix J.24

Specimen letter to agents of the company where agency agreements exist

Dear Sirs,

<u>   LIMITED IN RECEIVERSHIP</u>

I would advise you that my partner,   , and I were appointed joint administrative receivers of the above company on   by   Bank Plc under the terms of a debenture giving the holders a fixed and floating charge over the whole of the assets of the company.

I am at present enquiring into the affairs of the company and at the present time am unable to advise whether I wish the company to continue with the agency agreement. I hope to write to you again as soon as possible.

Please let me have a schedule of any of the company's property together with full details of any company monies that you are holding.

Yours truly,

Joint administrative receiver

150

Appendix J.25

Specimen letter to persons holding property of the company

Dear Sirs,

<u>LIMITED IN RECEIVERSHIP</u>

I would advise you that my partner,   , and I were appointed joint administrative receivers of the above company on   by   Bank Plc under the terms of a debenture giving the holders a fixed and floating charge over the whole of the assets of the company.

I enclose a copy of the deed by which I was appointed joint administrative receiver. I note that certain property of the company is held by you and should be grateful if you would confirm, by return, that these goods are held by you to my order and that no action in respect of these goods will be taken without my consent and authority.

Yours truly,

Joint administrative receiver

Appendix J.26

Specimen letter to companies in which the company holds shares

Dear Sirs,

<u>LIMITED IN RECEIVERSHIP</u>

I would advise you that my partner,   , and I were appointed joint administrative receivers of the above company on   by   Bank Plc under the terms of a debenture giving the holders a fixed and floating charge over the whole of the assets of the company.

I enclose a copy of the deed by which I was appointed joint administrative receiver and should be pleased if you would note my interest in the above company's shareholding in your company. You should also note that no transactions with regard to these shares are to take place without my approval and prior authority.

Please confirm that these instructions have been received and will be implemented.

Yours truly,

Joint administrative receiver

Appendix J.27

Specimen letter to persons having property on the company's premises

Dear Sirs,

<u>LIMITED IN RECEIVERSHIP</u>

I would advise you that my partner,   , and I were appointed joint administrative receivers of the above company on   by   Bank Plc under the terms of a debenture giving the holders a fixed and floating charge over the whole of the assets of the company.

I understand that certain property owned by you is at present on the company's premises. I have to advise you that the property is held by the company at your own risk and I can accept no liability whatsoever in this respect. Please advise as soon as possible concerning your intentions with regard to this property.

Yours truly,

Joint administrative receiver

Appendix J.28

Specimen letter to staff where the undertaking has been sold by the receiver

Dear Sirs,

<u>LIMITED IN RECEIVERSHIP</u>

I am writing to advise you that arrangements have now been made whereby
Limited, 'the purchasers', are purchasing the assets and undertaking of
Limited and will thus assume control of the business effective from

As a result of such sale I will not be requiring your services after   and
unfortunately you are accordingly redundant as from that date.* (However, after
consultation with the purchasers, I am hopeful that they will be able to offer you fresh
employment and would recommend that you should report to your place of work at
           a.m. on   to see if they are able so to do.)*

Under the provisions of the Employment Protection (Consolidation) Act 1978, any
claim which you may have for money in lieu of notice will, subject to certain
limitations, be paid to you by the Department of Employment out of the
Redundancy Fund. After the statutory minimum notice period to which you are
entitled has expired, please complete and return the form IP2 to the address shown.

You are required to mitigate as far as possible any claim for money in lieu of notice.
Consequently, if you are not offered fresh employment, you should ensure that you
obtain any social security benefits to which you may be entitled and make efforts to
obtain other employment.

Employees who have completed at least two years' continuous service with the
company and who are within the age limits laid down by the Employment Protection
(Consolidation) Act 1978, should qualify for redundancy pay. Payment of any
amount due to you cannot be made by the company and, therefore, your form RP21
should be addressed to the Department of Employment, Redundancy Payments
Office.

You are (are not) at liberty to disclose to the purchasers all information in your
possession relating to the business notwithstanding any terms of your employment
whether express or implied that would otherwise preclude you from so doing.

I would like to take this opportunity of thanking you for the co-operation which you
have afforded to me as joint administrative receiver and also to the company in the
past.

Yours truly,

Joint administrative receiver

154

Appendix J.29

Specimen letter to solicitors re: undertakings on sale of property

Dear Sirs,

<u>   LIMITED IN RECEIVERSHIP</u>

I am writing to confirm my instructions to you that you should act on my behalf in connection with the freehold/leasehold premises known as

My agents are   who have already provided me with a report on the property. Please refer any enquiries before contract direct to   in the first instance.

I understand that the property is charged to   Bank Plc, who hold the title deeds, and you may wish to provide the bank with a copy of this letter as your authority to act. In order to obtain the title deeds you will doubtless be required to give the bank an undertaking, and I should be grateful if you would ensure that any such undertaking recognises that any proceeds will be subject to the deduction of your own costs, those of my selling agents, and my own firm's costs where appropriate. Please let me have a copy of the undertaking for my file.

Yours truly,

Joint administrative receiver

Appendix J.30

Specimen letter to suppliers on sale of business and/or closure

Dear Sirs,

<u>LIMITED IN RECEIVERSHIP</u>

I am writing to advise you that the business and undertaking of   Limited was sold on

Accordingly, no further receivership orders will be issued and any future arrangements for the supply of goods must be made with the purchasers who are   Limited.

I would take this opportunity of thanking you for your support during the receivership trading period.

Yours truly,

Joint administrative receiver

156

Appendix J.31

Specimen letter to directors concerning tenancies

Dear Sirs,

<u>LIMITED IN RECEIVERSHIP</u>

The assets under my control as joint administrative receiver include the property at
. I now have to collect from those in occupation all moneys whether by
way of rent or otherwise arising out of the property and I should be grateful if you
would let me know immediately whether the occupants of the property have in any
way breached their lease or there is any other reason to doubt their right of
occupation.

Please also advise me immediately whether there is any further information of which
you think I should be aware concerning the property or the occupant thereof.

Yours truly,

Joint administrative receiver

Appendix J.32

Specimen letter to tenants

Dear Sirs,

<u>LIMITED IN RECEIVERSHIP</u>
(Address of property)

___

I would advise you that my partner,   , and I were appointed joint administrative receivers of the above company on   by   Bank Plc under the terms of a debenture giving the holders a fixed and floating charge over the whole of the assets of the company. A copy of the deed by which I was appointed is enclosed.

All rents, fees, compensation or other consideration or moneys payable in respect or arising out of any tenancy, licence or other basis upon which you occupy the above mentioned property must henceforth be paid to me or my duly authorised agent and not to any other person. However, neither by writing this letter nor by demanding or accepting any sums do I in any way create, confirm or adopt any lease, tenancy, licence or other right you may be claiming nor do I waive any breach of any obligation owed by you.

Yours truly,

Joint administrative receiver

Appendix J.33

Specimen letter to creditors re: VAT bad debt relief

TO ALL CREDITORS

Dear Sirs,

<u>   LIMITED IN RECEIVERSHIP</u>
<u>VAT BAD DEBT RELIEF</u>

On   I issued a certificate of insolvency for the purposes of Section 22(3)(b) of the Value Added Tax Act 1983 to the effect that, in my opinion, if it went into liquidation, the company's assets would be insufficient to cover the payment of any dividend in respect of debts which are neither preferential nor secured.

Creditors who are registered with H M Customs and Excise for VAT purposes and whose claims against the company include any sums charged for value added tax should now be able to claim VAT bad debt relief. You do not need to produce a copy of the certificate but this letter should be retained with your VAT records as evidence of its issue.

Yours truly,

Joint administrative receiver

Appendix J.34

Specimen letter: indemnity by company

THIS DEED OF INDEMNITY is made the   day of
198   BETWEEN   LIMITED (In Liquidation) ('the company')
acting by   of   ('the liquidator') of the one part and
of   ('the receiver') of the other part

WHEREAS:-

(A)   The administrative receiver was on   198   appointed administrative receiver of all the property comprised in a debenture issued by the company to
          ('the debenture holder') on   198   .

(B)   The liquidator was appointed liquidator of the company (by order of the
Court) (a resolution passed at a meeting of the members/creditors of the company
held) on   198   .

NOW IT IS HEREBY AGREED as follows:

1.   THE company acting by the liquidator hereby undertakes and agrees with the
receiver that the company will as a liability in its liquidation at all times hereafter
indemnify and keep indemnified the receiver and any person who at the request or
under the direction of the receiver has been or becomes engaged in the conduct of the
receivership from and against any liability falling upon the receiver or any such
person as aforesaid arising out of the reasonable and proper conduct of the
receivership and without prejudice to the generality of the foregoing all or any of the
following namely:

1.1   any liability falling upon the receiver under Sections 37 or 40 of the Insolvency
      Act 1986;
1.2   any liability to a creditor of the company claiming to be secured or asserting
      reservation of title or to a purchaser of the subject-matter of such a claim or
      assertion;
1.3   any other liability incurred or suffered by the receiver or any such person as
      aforesaid in the reasonable and proper conduct of the receivership;
1.4   any proper fee commission or expense to which the receiver may be or may
      become or but for his discharge as receiver would have been entitled;

but in each case to the extent only that such liability could have properly been
discharged out of assets remaining in the receiver's hands had he not handed them
over to the liquidator.

PROVIDED THAT the company shall not be liable under the terms of this Deed of
Indemnity for sums in excess of assets remaining in the hands of the liquidator at the
date on which written notice claiming such indemnity is given by the receiver to the
liquidator after the liquidator has paid or satisfied all proper fees charged and
expenses and liabilities to third parties incurred by the liquidator or by the company
in question.

2.   THIS DEED shall inure for the benefit of successors assigns and personal
representations of the receiver and any such person as aforesaid and be binding upon
the successors in office and assigns of the liquidator.

3.   THE company acting by the liquidator undertakes upon reasonable notice to
give to the receiver or persons nominated by him access to the books, documents and

records of the company for so long as the liquidator is obliged by law to retain or retains custody thereof.

4.   THE company acting by its liquidator undertakes to give the receiver no less than 21 days prior notice of his intention to declare a dividend to any class of creditors.

5.   THIS Deed shall be without prejudice to any right of indemnity to which by law the receiver or any such person as aforesaid is entitled.

IN WITNESS whereof the liquidator has caused the common seal of the company to be hereunto affixed the day and year first above written.

THE COMMON SEAL of
                                          LIMITED
was hereunto affixed in the
presence of:

                                          Liquidator

Appendix J.35

Specimen letter to request advertisement of notice of meeting of creditors

Dear Sirs,

<u>LIMITED IN RECEIVERSHIP</u>

Further to my appointment as joint administrative receiver of the above company, I enclose the notice of the meeting of creditors to be advertised in the London Gazette and in a local paper circulating in the company's main place of business. [See appendix I.5].

Please submit your invoice in the normal way.

Yours truly,

Joint administrative receiver

Appendix K.1

Specimen instructions to the Finance Director/Company Secretary

Dear

<u>LIMITED IN RECEIVERSHIP</u>

I should be grateful if you would *urgently* deal with the following:

1.   Ensure that all credit cards have been collected and credit account facilities cancelled as at the date of the receivership appointment. All credit cards should be given to my representative with an accompanying schedule of cardholders.

2.   Provide details of all directors and employees holding service contracts.

3.   Provide the receivers with copies of the latest audited and management accounts.

4.   Confirm the location of the company seal and provide the receivers with a copy of the Memorandum and Articles, together with the company's Minute Book(s).

5.   Liaise with production regarding the preparation of schedules relating to completion of work-in-progress.

6.   Prepare, within the next 48 hours, a weekly cash flow for the next 12 weeks with a final column indicating the debtor/creditor position at the end of the period.

   Pre-receivership debtor receipts should be excluded. Receivership sales receipts should be shown as being received within the normal credit terms granted by the company, whereas purchases should be shown as being paid within seven days of receipt of the goods. Both sales and purchasing requirements should be included on the basis of the instructions given to the respective departments, copies of which are attached.

   Wages and salaries should be included *gross* to include National Insurance and VAT should be shown as a separate liability payable *monthly*. Remember to include the immediate cash requirement for wages and salaries.

7.   Prepare and/or implement the following, indicating book values where relevant:

   (i) A full physical check of stock and work-in-progress noting the value of any provisions made for obsolete and slow-moving items. Specifically note those stocks subject to reservation of title and work-in-progress held by sub-contracts, indicating the amounts owed to the suppliers concerned.

   (ii) A schedule of the company's freehold and leasehold properties together with details and copies of all leases, licence agreements and recent valuations.

   (iii) An inventory of plant and machinery, indicating all items on hire purchase or lease and the name of the finance company. Provide copies of any recent valuations.

(iv) A schedule of insurance policies currently in force, together with copies of those policies.

(v) Details of pension schemes indicating trustees, administrators and whether over-funded or not.

(vi) A schedule setting out the details of any quoted or unquoted investments held by the company, assets held by third parties in bond or otherwise and details of any assets which have been written down to nil in the company's books but which may be of value.

(vii) A schedule of any licences, patents, royalty, trading or agency agreements granted to or by other parties relevant to the company's own operations.

(viii) A schedule of any investment grants or other Government grants which have been received, the terms of which reserve the right of title to any equipment purchases as a result of such grants (e.g. Ministry of Defence contracts).

(ix) A summary of the current tax position in respect of outstanding Corporation Tax, tax deducted from interest payable, tax on Capital Gains, ACT or Development Land Tax, together with any other relevant tax matters.

(x) A summary of claims which the company may have against any suppliers or claims against customers which are in liquidation or receivership.

(xi) The statutory statement of affairs required under Section 47 of the Insolvency Act 1986, the documentation for which will be provided by my manager.

(xii) A summary of any other matters which you feel should be brought to my attention.

Yours truly,

Joint administrative receiver

Copy instructions attached re: Sales
                                  Purchasing
                                  Production
                                  Accounts
                                  Wages/Personnel

Appendix K.2

Specimen instructions to the Finance Director/Company Secretary

Dear Sir,

<u>   LIMITED IN RECEIVERSHIP</u>

As you are aware, my partner,   , and I were appointed joint administrative receivers of the above company on   by   Bank Plc under the terms of a debenture giving the holders a fixed and floating charge over the whole of the assets of the company.

I should be grateful if you would provide me as soon as possible with the following schedules, showing in each case, where applicable, which assets are the subject of retention of title clauses, hire purchase contracts, charges, garnishees or any other encumbrance. The schedule should also show, where applicable, the approximate book values together with estimated realisable valuations. The schedules I require are as follows:

(a)   Cash balances at offices and depots.
(b)   Balances at banks.
(c)   Book debts (aged) and other receivables.
(d)   Licences, patents, royalty or agency agreements granted to, or by, other parties.
(e)   Investment grants or other Government grants received or to be received.
(f)   Freehold and leasehold land and buildings.
(g)   Stocks and work-in-progress. (A physical check should be carried out.)
(h)   Listed securities.
(i)   Investments in other companies, including subsidiaries.
(j)   Any other assets.
(k)   Particulars of all items which are on the company's premises but which are not the property of the company including goods supplied under reserved title.
(l)   Assets not on company's premises, owned by the company.
(m) Uncalled capital.
(n)   Preferential creditors (estimated if necessary).
(o)   The current tax position.
(p)   A list of staff.

The books of accounts should be completely written up and balanced as at the date of my appointment. New ledger accounts should be opened in the personal ledgers to record all post receivership transactions and for the time being all other records are to be maintained.

Please advise me forthwith in the event of any difficulties and I will endeavour to arrange assistance for you.

Yours truly,

Joint administrative receiver

Appendix K.3

Specimen instructions to the accounts department

To the Accounts Department

<u>IN RECEIVERSHIP</u>

The joint administrative receivers have requested that the following instructions be implemented forthwith:

(i) Advise all credit card companies and/or suppliers or garages providing credit account facilities that all such facilities must be cancelled as at the date of the receiver's appointment.

(ii) Prepare a list of the names and addresses of all known creditors of the company as soon as possible. The amount owing is *not* important. Include credit balances on sales ledger.

(iii) Provide the receivers with copies and details of all outstanding accounts in respect of rent, rates, electricity and gas, with details of the periods to which the outstanding payments are applicable.

(iv) Prepare a schedule of all hire purchase and leasing agreements indicating:
    (a) The leasing company and the agreement number.
    (b) The assets to which the agreement refers.
    (c) The date of the agreement, the monthly/quarterly charge, and the number of months to completion, or secondary leasing period. In the case of leasing agreements state whether there is a purchase option.

(v) As soon as possible, prepare an aged schedule of outstanding debtors showing the anticipated week of receipt. Also indicate bad and doubtful debts and possible contra items or disputes. All debtor balances outstanding at the date of the receivers' appointment should be brought up to date and statements issued to customers.

(vi) Provide details of employee expenses outstanding indicating petty cash floats held by employees. Also provide details of employee loans or amounts outstanding in respect of staff accounts as well as cash deposits held by third parties.

(vii) Prepare the relevant VAT returns up to the date of the receivers' appointment and advise them of the amount outstanding.

(viii) The following accounting procedure should be followed during the receivership:
    (a) Existing books of account should be drawn off leaving a space for outstanding transactions to be recorded. The writing up of cash books, sales ledger, wages records and stock records should be maintained subject to the comments below. In the case of contracting companies the relevant contract records should also be maintained.
    (b) Cash received after the date of the receivers' appointment should be recorded on a daily basis and divided clearly on a column basis between pre-receivership and post-receivership debtors.
    (c) Details of all cheques drawn and requiring the receivers' signatures must be entered on the prescribed requisition forms together with supporting documents. These forms can be obtained from the receivers' representative and copies should be sent on a daily basis to the accounts department at the relevant office.
    (d) All cheques, when despatched, should have attached a standard note to
    N.B. the effect that the cheque is provided on the understanding that the recipient will not apply set-off in respect of monies due to him prior to the receivers' appointment.

(e) The cash book should be maintained on a daily basis and a weekly analysis prepared. *Each day* the closing balance for the previous night together with details of cash received on the day in question should be given to the receivers' representative.

(f) Sales invoicing should be done on a weekly basis and a check should be made to ensure that, where applicable, written confirmation has been received from customers.

(g) Prepare trading accounts every four weeks and if feasible a stock check should be carried out.

(ix) *Please note* that all outgoing documentation and correspondence must have the words 'in receivership' after the company's name, the name of the appointed administrative receivers and the date of appointment.

If there are any queries arising in respect of these instructions, please consult with the receivers as soon as possible.

Appendix K.4

Specimen instructions to the personnel and wages department

To Personnel and Wages Department

<u>   LIMITED IN RECEIVERSHIP</u>

The joint administrative receivers have requested that the following instructions be implemented forthwith:

(i) Advise the receivers or their manager as soon as possible of the immediate requirements for wages and salaries during the next five days. Please provide gross amount *plus* NI and net requirement.

(ii) Provide a schedule of all company employees categorised by skill or location and indicating gross salary/weekly wage including normal overtime, applicable NI, national insurance number and date of commencing employment. This schedule should be given to the receivers as soon as possible.

(iii) Calculate the monthly amount of PAYE and national insurance contributions unpaid at the date of the receivers' appointment giving the due date.

(iv) Provide details of employee and employer pension contributions unpaid at the date of appointment, up to a maximum of 12 months in arrears, as well as outstanding deductions for union dues, holiday and sickness funds, etc. Include amounts outstanding re holiday pay entitlements for the current holiday year only.

(v) Prepare P35s, P11ds and, if applicable, Forms SC35 for sub-contractor's tax. Give sub-contractor's certificate issued to the company to the receivers' representative.

(vi) Provide details of any protective awards or other industrial tribunal claims.

(vii) *Please note* that all outgoing documentation and correspondence must have the words 'in receivership' after the company's name, the names of the appointed administrative receivers and the date of appointment.

If there are any queries arising in respect of these instructions, please consult the receivers or their representative immediately.

Appendix K.5

Specimen instructions to the purchasing department

To Purchasing Department

<u>LIMITED IN RECEIVERSHIP</u>

The joint administrative receivers have requested that the following instructions be implemented forthwith:

    (i) No goods are to be accepted into the warehouse without the receivers' approval.

    (ii) All existing orders should be regarded as cancelled unless alternative arrangements are made *in writing* by the receivers.

    (iii) Advise the receivers immediately on receipt of any writs, walking possession orders or petitions issued against the company.

    (iv) Provide the receivers as a matter of urgency with a summary of those suppliers who have, to your knowledge, a reservation of title clause in their conditions of sale, or who have supplied goods as consignment or sale or return.

    (v) Ascertain the approximate value of unused goods in stock applicable to the relevant suppliers and the current amount outstanding to them. *Likewise*, provide details of sub-contractors holding company goods, indicating the value of the current job and the total amount outstanding to that sub-contractor.

    (vi) As soon as possible, and after consultation with the sales department and factory production control, provide the receivers with a schedule of immediate requirements for the next 8-12 weeks on the assumption that existing stocks will be used where possible until such time as they have been reduced to a 4 week stockholding. Divide requirements between those needed to complete current work-in-progress and those required for new, unstarted orders. Indicate on a weekly basis stock reductions.

    (vii) Orders should only be issued for requirements on a 2-4 week rolling basis unless 'lead times' dictate otherwise and subject to (vi) above re stockholding. In these circumstances, the receivers should be consulted.

    (viii) A new sequence of order numbers should be started, together with the prefix *REC*. All orders must be signed by the receivers or their representative and the copy order should be marked up with the approximate value of the order.

Appendix K.6

Specimen instructions to the sales and despatch department

To Sales & Despatch Department

<u>   LIMITED IN RECEIVERSHIP</u>

The joint administrative receivers have requested that the following instructions be implemented forthwith:

N.B.

(i) Confirm details of any transport company currently carrying or warehousing goods over which they may be able to claim a lien. If any such case exists, advise the receivers immediately with the amount owing to each transporter and the value of goods held by them. *Do not use* such a transporter until approval has been obtained from the receivers.

(ii) Ensure that all sales representatives are aware of the receivership. Advise them that all credit cards have been cancelled and that cash floats will be provided where required. Request them to forward details of unpaid expenses outstanding at the date of the receivers' appointment for consideration.

(iii) Provide a schedule of all sales representatives indicating their sales area of responsibility. Detail agents engaged for both home and overseas territories.

(iv) Provide the receivers, the purchasing department and factory production as soon as possible with a summary of the current sales order position, indicating the value to be despatched and invoiced to sales over the next 12 weeks and thereafter on a weekly basis. List major sales customers.

(v) Indicate the value of orders already in work-in-progress and those which are as yet unstarted. Liaise with factory production control.

(vi) It should be noted that the company may continue selling its products subject to the following conditions:

(a) Where goods are being supplied under a long term running contract, no goods should be supplied until such time as the customer has accepted *in writing* to the receivers or by telex that continuation of such supply does *not* constitute an adoption of that contract by the receivers. The receivers should be given details of any such contracts immediately.

(b) No goods should be supplied to a customer who is also a *creditor* of the company until he has agreed *in writing* to the receivers or by telex not to hold goods against monies due to him *prior* to the receivers' appointment. Ask the receivers' representative for a specimen letter to be sent to such customers.

Appendix K.7

Specimen instructions to factory production

To Factory Production

LIMITED IN RECEIVERSHIP

The joint administrative receivers have requested that the following instructions be implemented forthwith:

(i) Do not accept goods into the factory unless authorised by the receivers and/or their representative or unless they have been supplied against a receivership order signed by the receivers.

(ii) Prepare a schedule of current contracts, indicating orders in work-in-progress and orders issued into production but not yet started. Indicate those jobs where disputes exist, together with details thereof.

(iii) Prepare anticipated production schedules for the next 12 weeks on the assumption that new orders will only be started if they are capable of completion within a 12 week period from the date of the receivership appointment. Identify those work-in-progress orders which will not be completed within the period.

(iv) Prepare a schedule of work-in-progress, indicating the sales value of each job; the cost of labour, sub-contract work and materials to complete; retentions if relevant, and payments received to date. Indicate those materials which are in stock and those which need to be ordered, including outside processing. This information must be prepared on a contract by contract basis where applicable.

(v) Take stock at the date of the receivers' appointment re finished goods, raw materials, parts and work-in-progress. This should be done in liaison with the Finance Director. Obsolescent, obsolete and slow-moving items should be *separately* identified. Values should be attributed to all the stock on the basis of the lower of cost or net realisable value.

(vi) Advise the purchasing department with regard to materials and sub-contract requirements over the coming 12 weeks on the assumption that stock levels
N.B. must be reduced to no more than a 4 week holding. *Advise immediately of urgent items required within the next 7 days.*

(vii) Identify any problems which are known to exist with regard to reservation of title or consignment goods, or where goods are held by sub-contractors who are owed money. Include any tool-makers where tooling is held and required for production over the next 12 weeks. Also identify any 'lead time' problems. Liaise with the purchasing department.

(viii) Prepare a schedule of the numbers of employees required to meet the production schedules for the next 12 weeks, indicating the numbers in each category required.

(ix) Cease all work on research and development, guarantee work or non-essential machine rebuilding and maintenance until agreed by the receivers. Prepare a schedule of what is currently in progress on these matters.

(x) Identify any current problems with plant and machinery and provide estimates of costs to rectify. Also provide a schedule of those items of plant which are either on hire purchase or lease.

(xi) *Please note* that all outgoing documentation and correspondence must have the words 'in receivership' after the company's name, the names of the appointed joint administrative receivers and the date of appointment.

(xii) No goods may be ordered without the approval of the receivers accompanied by an order signed by the receivers or their representative.

Appendix K.8

Specimen instructions to the transport department

To Transport Department

_____ LIMITED IN RECEIVERSHIP

The joint administrative receivers have requested that the following instructions be implemented forthwith:

   (i) Prepare a schedule of those vehicles which are undergoing repair at an independent garage for which payment has *not* yet been made. If possible, give an estimate of the cost of repair.
  (ii) Provide a schedule of all vehicles owned by the company, the name of the driver and whether on hire purchase or lease. Give name of leasing or hire purchase company concerned.
 (iii) Advise all drivers that credit cards and credit account facilities have been cancelled and arrange with the receivers the cash floats to be provided or alternative arrangements made.
  (iv) *Please note* that all outgoing documentation and correspondence must have the words 'in receivership' after the company's name, the names of the appointed administrative receivers and the date of appointment.

Appendix K.9

Specimen instructions to the estimating and contracts department (Building and Construction companies only)

To Estimating and Contracts department

<u>LIMITED IN RECEIVERSHIP</u>

The joint administrative receivers have requested that the following instructions be implemented forthwith:

(i) Arrangements should be made immediately for all sites to be adequately secured.

(ii) Provide the receivers with a schedule of the foreman in charge of each site and the number of men on site.

(iii) The receivers have appointed   & Co to prepare a schedule of all existing contracts, together with details showing costs to date, works certified and paid, outstanding certificates, cost to complete and net asset value. They will also require details of nominated sub-contractors and monies outstanding to such contractors. You are requested to provide all assistance to them in preparing these schedules.

(iv) Contract employers and/or main contractors are being approached with a request to provide the company with 14-21 days grace in order to try and arrange an assignment of the relevant contracts to new contractors.

(v) No work should proceed on any contract until such time as the exercise has been completed. Where it is decided to continue on a particular contract, it will be on a week to week basis as agreed in writing between   & Co and the relevant employer/main contractor or relevant sub-contractors.

Appendix K.10

Specimen instructions to company accounts department/other relevant departments (if business hived down)

To Company Accounts department
    Other relevant departments

<u>   LIMITED IN RECEIVERSHIP</u>

A new company has been formed to assist the joint administrative receivers in disposing of the undertaking of the company's business.

With effect from   , all sales will be undertaken through
Limited trading as   . Accordingly, the following should be implemented:

  (i) All despatch notes, invoices and statements should be amended to reflect the new company, i.e. delete 'Limited' after   Limited and insert, in line with the attached specimen, prop   Limited (a rubber stamp would be of assistance).

 (ii) A new VAT number has been obtained which should be noted on all sales documentation, including quotations, etc. Also the company number,   , should be included on all relevant correspondence.

(iii) All outgoing sales correspondence which relates to transactions entered into after the above date should be amended in accordance with (i) above.

(iv) New books of account should be started, including cash book and sales ledger.

 (v) Sales receipts relating to sales after   must be paid into the   Limited bank account.

Index

(Note: references to 'administrative receivers' have been shown below as 'receivers')

References are to paragraph numbers